W9-ATA-276

# Collectors' Guide to
# Antique American Glass

# Collectors'
# Guide to

Iridescent glass vase. Tiffany Favrile
glass, circa 1900. *The Brooklyn Museum
Collection.*

# Antique American
# Glass

## by Marvin D. Schwartz

Doubleday & Company, Inc., Garden City, New York

# Preface

This book was written for you if you are curious about the fuss some people make about American glass, if you are a collector who has, thus far, concentrated his attention on one single phase of the subject and want to see where it fits into the general history of glass, or if you are a student of Americana who would like to see how glass relates to the rest of the decorative arts. Intentionally simple, written for the beginning collector, this book surveys the entire field of American glass briefly in the chapters that follow.

This book will not supply the names of the infinite number of factories that were actively producing glass between 1608 and now, but rather is one that chronicles the styles and the approaches to both glass and design that are encountered on the American scene. In glassmaking as in the other crafts, there is both consistency and variety in the design of any nation, and American expression was distinctive from a surprisingly early period.

American glass is a fascinating subject and particularly rich in revealing facets of American economic and esthetic development. The study of glass is helpful in developing an appreciation of the diverse ambitions and tastes that have influenced American growth. Glass, more than the other decorative arts, has grown with the country especially as the industry supplied goods to satisfy esthetic demands, for it reflected the growing middle classes and their tastes. Some of the designs that were most questionable in taste were executed in faultless techniques suited to the needs of a people who were searching for new concepts and tradition at the same time.

In this introduction to the subject, the many tendencies of American glass are discussed and the many techniques and approaches are described in a stylistic evolution.

For many collectors, there is an overemphasis on the object and its authenticity without concern for its place in the history of art. Often a collector is at opposite poles from the student who would concentrate on the context from which the object comes, not the object itself. In this guide for the beginning collector it is the student approach that is taken in the hope of providing the collector with some of the information that he generally overlooks. It is a broad survey of the history of American glass that shows the beginning collector how to consider the objects he has acquired in their context.

# Contents

# Introduction

Glass manufacture has been a challenge to men since very ancient times because it is a product of man's ingenuity and hand skills. The glassmaker takes a bit of sand and a few other ingredients and, handling them properly, produces a transparent product of amazing qualities. It is the perfect container for a variety of liquids, it is beautiful, and it can be as valuable as a precious metal or stone when it is finely made.

Considering the gains possible, it is not surprising to find that for centuries many were willing to risk large amounts of capital to establish glassmaking establishments in as unlikely a place as seventeenth-century Virginia. Although the results of the early efforts in Virginia are not properly known, they did mark the beginning of a long history of American glass, a medium that appealed as much for esthetic as functional reasons.

*The Origin of the American Glass Industry*

When the colonies were first settled there was some question about what their role should be. Originally it was thought that manufacturing would be a good enterprise. The settlement coincided with an experimental period of glassmaking in England and the discovery that not just any sand would do for the manufacture of fine glass. When it was discovered that the sand of Virginia was right for the best glassmaking, an industry was founded which was later to grow to large proportions. Probably the glasshouses active in the seventeenth century in the American colonies concentrated their efforts on making functional products, but there was some more decorative work done, and perhaps the time may come when that will be uncovered.

*American Glass Research*

American glass history falls into two categories at this point in research. There is a documentary history that provides information on the glasshouses that existed and gives us some idea about the number of them and the character of the operation. Then there is a group of glass objects that have survived which can be associated with American production. A good part of the American glass that is known has been identified with one or another glasshouse, but more often than not the identification is on the basis of association and "second thoughts" than on the more readily confirmed uses of bills of sale or inscriptions. There is still a long way to go before the earliest history of American glass can be definitive.

*Distinctive American Glass*

American glass ranges from the simple to the elaborate but somehow despite the broad scope and many variations in design there seems to be a discernible consistency. No matter what style or how fussy a piece may be there is a certain directness representing the designer's attempting to keep forms clear and functional. Glass is a particularly interesting field of inquiry in design because it became a vehicle of popular art that was enormously appealing to the growing middle-class taste of the late nineteenth century. In the nineteenth century when skills were less evident in the majority of work done in silver and furniture, glass and ceramics remained vehicles for fine technical expression. Curiously enough in the field of glass the distinctive American product remained important and skillful, if occasionally a little revolting to serious estheticians.

In surveying American glass here, the emphasis has been on the material that would fall into the category of decorative art rather than on glass production as a whole. In seeking out the available material, the late eighteenth century would seem to mark the beginning of the tradition that is known today. Securely dated material is from the 1760s at the earliest and more likely dates closer to 1770.

There is a marked relationship between the American products and the products of lesser or provincial glasshouses of the continent and England. The connections that become evident at first are with conservative provincial fashions and the peasant tradition. In the simple blown pieces decorated with floral designs either in enamel or engraved there is a strong connection with peasant glass and although the German houses come to mind, many other centers produced these wares. In colored molded pieces, the forms reflected the light Oriental models favored by fashionable designers of the rococo style, which was the vogue between about 1740 and 1780 on the American scene. After the Revolution, there was a shift in taste which brought a revival of more faithful use of Greco-Roman ornament, a beginning of the sense of a historic awareness in the arts and this is partly evident in work on the American scene. In this period simple decorative decanters and goblets were made which confirm the notion of American work being more functional.

## The Americanization of European Glass Techniques

In the Post-Revolutionary period, bottle and window glass manufacture increased. Craftsmen in the proliferation of glasshouses popping up all over the country made tablewares as a sideline, which were sometimes playful attempts at elegance and other times purely utilitarian, but always made of the

metal used for bottles and windows. There were
reflections of current fashion in that work, but
more important was the fact that it was traditional
and an opportunity for glassmakers to show off their
abilities. Known as offhand work, this glass was
a medium of folk expression. In it fine early techniques are encountered in interpretations for rural
consumers of the nineteenth century. Delicate "latticinio" became broad striping in looped glass,
and Venetian techniques for modeling in molten
glass were simplified to produce a chicken finial or
crude linear pattern.

*The Expansion*   In spite of the difficulties glassmakers encountered
*of the Industry*  the growing group of glasshouses had ambitious
aims. Fine cut glass was made in a number of
early nineteenth-century glasshouses. In Pittsburgh
and the east fine flint glass was produced and cut in
the latest neoclassical fashion. Based on ancient
Greco-Roman models, cut glass was quite different
from the relief-ornamented early models. The inexpensive imitation, blown three-mold glass was actually much closer to the ancient originals than cut
glass. Surfaces were in lower relief in both the ancient work and the molded nineteenth-century examples than in the more elaborate version.

Another new technique developed in the 1820s
involved making pressed glass. The moldmaker was
the creative artist; the glassblower simply had the
responsibility of applying his skills in pouring the
molten metal into molds. Pressed glass came into
its own after 1830 with elaborate over-all patterns
that hid imperfections. The Empire style, the late
version of neoclassicism which was in fashion from
about 1815 to 1850, was an important source of
design. Rococo and Gothic revival ornament also
played a significant role in early pressed glass which

is popularly called "Lacy glass." Americans produced the best of this type; seemingly they knew how to use an over-all pattern without making it too complex. European pressed glass, which was made in imitation of the American product, is generally unmistakable because it is not as successful. On the other hand, by the 1840s Americans working in cut glass found new sources of inspiration in the colored cased glass that was perfected in Bohemia. Cased glass was made by putting a layer of color on clear glass and cutting it out to create clear and colored designs which were in the rococo or Renaissance revival styles.

*From a Craft to an Art*

After the middle of the nineteenth century there was a full range of decorative techniques to be found in American glass. Small glasshouses produced the folk product. Cut and pressed glass were made by the larger manufacturers in the east and Midwest. The constant arrival of skilled labor from foreign shores provided a substitute for apprenticeship and was the source of new ideas. The introduction of fine decorative work by the English and continental manufacturers began to have its effect on the American scene in the 1850s but was not really important until the 1880s. It is interesting to see how quickly the European craftsmen were assimilated. Their work became characteristically American after a relatively short time. Art glass was a phenomenon of importance in being a completely popular attempt at pretension which showed off the skills of the craftsmen in designs that reflected the latest efforts at seeking out new techniques. It was the 1890s before a really artistic effort was made in art glass when Louis Comfort Tiffany began making Favrile glass in the Art Nouveau style. Much that followed in the early part of the century reflected the decoration of Tiffany without exploiting his experimental philosophy.

Throughout the evolution of American glass, changes in style did not affect the approach to the medium evident in the American factories. Even the constant revitalization of the houses by skilled immigrants never reduced the characteristically American elements in the native products.

the sources of Stiegel design because there is European peasant work mixed with the American work.

## Modern Revivals

Another area of innocent confusion at times is the modern glass made at glasshouses in the early spirit. Mexican glasshouses stand out as refuges for early techniques and their wares have caused confusion. Czech glasshouses were able to reproduce Stiegel-like perfume bottles in the 1920s, but the thought is that it was made in an attempt to fake. A blown-glass operation which exploits eighteenth- and nineteenth-century techniques is still going strong outside of Venice. There a number of small shops have survived and several of these make reproductions of art glass for the American market that have been passed off as originals.

## Fakes

Every type of glass that has appealed to collectors has attracted the copyists. Blown three-mold forms and pressed-glass fakes turn up from time to time. Many of the most confusing are forty years old, but although these now show wear, they somehow look less convincing than they did when new. A new trick today is to apply fake names to twentieth-century work that may be signed. Kits with the familiar marks of Steuben, Lalique, and Tiffany are available for unscrupulous dealers to etch on decent unmarked glass. The faker is generally about 80 percent correct and the 20 percent error becomes more evident as time passes.

## The Necessity for Study

Every enthusiastic collector has been fooled at least once. When he acts on impulse he only hopes he sees what he wants, but he sometimes finds he has missed. Nevertheless the best way to avoid error is to study by looking and by reading. Most major museums have glass collections. Most important for

# CHAPTER I

# How to Be a Wary Collector

Glass collecting is difficult because of the problems in determining the authenticity of a piece. There are intentional fakes, reproductions confused with the original, and contemporary examples not made where they were thought to have been made which may be taken for authentic work. To avoid the pitfalls it is important to exercise caution and to begin by being a very conservative collector. Most fakes differ from the original in many ways and are accepted as original because they seem logical variations. By studying public collections, one can develop a proper idea of what to expect. Ascertaining age in glass is challenging because wear is the single sign of it. Design is often determined by aspects of the technique which make it difficult to use design as a criterion of period. Good old glass has a ring that most of the reproductions lack.

*The Most Important Error*    The first error for the collector who would be a connoisseur is in attributing European glass to American glasshouses. This can be avoided by sticking closely to the models that compare with the better known examples. When collectors began showing their enthusiasm for American glass, some dealers felt it their obligation to supply the demand and they did so by buying whatever "looked" American in Germany, Czechoslovakia, Spain, France, and England. Now it has become very difficult to decide serious glass collectors are those of the Corning Museum, the Toledo Museum, the Metropolitan Museum of Art, the Wadsworth Athenaeum, the Henry Ford Museum, the Brooklyn Museum, Detroit Institute of Arts, all of which approach the subject of glass generally. For art glass in particular, the Bennington Museum and the Chrysler Art Museum of Provincetown, Massachusetts, offer broad groups of glass.

Further study should begin with *American Glass* by George S. and Helen McKearin which was published first in 1941. The same authors also wrote *Two Hundred Years of American Blown Glass.* There are books on special subjects by Ruth Webb Lee that show aspects of nineteenth-century pressed glass, and studies by A. C. Revi on art glass and later pressed glass, cut glass, and bottles. Dorothy Daniels, *Cut and Engraved Glass 1771–1905* surveys American examples. The literature for collectors is constantly growing. Serious brief studies appear in *The Journal of Glass* which is published annually by the Corning Museum. *Antiques* magazine has the longest and best record as the source of new information on glass. They have published the fruits of excavations since the '30s and detailed glass research since their inception so that going through back issues with the aid of the indices that are available will be most helpful.

Glass study may be very rewarding if observation of important pieces is coupled with reading about them. Collecting information and perceptions is as important as buying.

# CHAPTER II

# American Glass: Techniques and Chronology

American glass is a field broad in scope and varied in design. Made in small shops and large factories, the designs were determined by the limitations of the glassblower or the moldmaker. Notwithstanding the variety of designs, there has been a consistency to American glass that makes it possible to identify it easily. American glass design, no matter how fussy, is more functional than its European equivalents.

The American glassblower of the seventeenth century and rural craftsmen as late as 1900 concentrated on making simple "bottle" window glass in aquamarine, green, olive, or amber. Glass, a combination of silicas (sand) and alkalis fired at high temperatures, turns the "bottle" colors because of impurities in the materials. This type of glass is traditionally called green glass and has a heavy rustic appearance. In the eighteenth century when clear glass was made it was most often a glass of soda made of purer materials. One type of clear glass, popularly called flint glass, is made with oxide of lead. This had been introduced in England late in the seventeenth century and made at American glasshouses after 1760 along with colored glass made by adding a coloring agent such as a metallic oxide.

| | |
|---|---|
| *Variety of Techniques* | One basic method of making glass is by forming it with a blowpipe. The molten metal is picked up in a gather, and the craftsman literally blows a bubble |

of glass to form a vessel. A variety of shapes can be made depending upon the skill of the blower and the quality of the metal. The finished product may be smooth, clear, and flawless or relatively rough. It might be decorated by adding extra gathers of glass as a border while the piece is still hot or by cutting or engraving or painting after it has cooled.

A technique for creating relief patterns was particularly popular in the eighteenth and early nineteenth centuries. This involved blowing the molten metal through a so-called expand-mold. A regular repeating design was enlarged as the metal was blown; the farther it got from the mold the larger the motif became.

After the American Revolution, American-made lead glass, also called flint glass, was improved. This was a purer product than the ordinary clear glass and lent itself to cut-glass work.

The nineteenth century saw development in manufacturing techniques. Full-size molds were devised. For the first type the glass was blown into the mold to create relief patterns that were bold in scale. Soon after, pressed-glass molds were introduced. For pressing, the gather of glass was put in the mold and pressure was applied. At first, from 1830 to 1840, intricate patterns were typical of pressed glass, but not later. Nineteenth-century competition inspired the development of inexpensive lime glass.

*Variety of Styles*

At first American glass was an interesting cross between fashionable and folk art. American work attributed to the eighteenth century is a result of the combination of English and German approaches. On the one hand there was the traditionalism of German peasant art. On the other hand was the provincial stylishness of the lesser English houses in Bristol and other port towns, an influence that led to the use of expand-mold, diamond-patterned sugar bowls, and the like. As time went on, current fashions played more of a role. For example, in the early nineteenth century the various phases of neoclassical style affected the designs of the molded wares. Later, each succeeding fashion was a source of inspiration for glassmakers.

# CHAPTER III

# The European Background of American Glass

American glassmakers always depended upon European craftsmen for new ideas and new fashions, but they assimilated these into work that was distinctive.

*Venice: the Glassmaking Center*

When the American colonies were first settled in the seventeenth century, Venice was the undisputed center of the production of fine glassware. Glassmakers from Venice worked in cities all over Europe, thus spreading its influence. Venetian glass was stylish, delicate, and a product of obvious skill. It was what all glasshouses hoped to achieve. The Venetian craftsmen employed a variety of techniques to produce their wares, and by the seventeenth century they had centuries of tradition behind them. Clear and colored glass were used in forms based on classical models. The striated glass, called latticinio, was a favorite Venetian type. The plain examples were often decorated with engraving. Venetian design was very much an expression of the virtuosity of the glassblower. The forms used generally reflected the Baroque style which flourished from about 1600 to 1700. This style is most simply

Three Venetian goblets, seventeenth century. *The Brooklyn Museum Collection.*

Latticinio bottle, Venetian, seventeenth century. *The Brooklyn Museum Collection.*

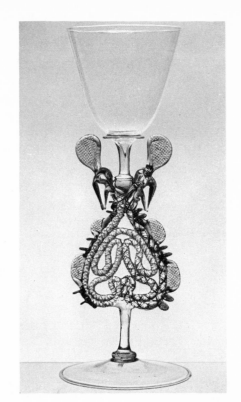

Venetian-type winged goblet, Low Countries, seventeenth century. *The Brooklyn Museum Collection.*

defined as a phase of the revival of classical art in which designs are arranged in rhythmical patterns to suggest movement.

*Glass in the Netherlands*

The Lowlands craftsmen of the seventeenth century made glass in a native decorative tradition as well as following Venetian fashion. The green "roemer," with a tall cylindrical lower section decorated with applied prunts of glass and a globular upper section, was characteristic. Northern glass was traditionally heavy and green. After they began copying the Venetians, the Dutch evolved a special style of engraving.

One characteristic product of the German glasshouses was the tall cylindrical beaker with painted decoration which inspired peasant ware.

Wine goblet, Dutch or German, circa 1700. *The Brooklyn Museum Collection.*

*England*

English glassmaking was transformed in the course of the seventeenth century from producing simple utilitarian wares to attempting to work in fashion. Italian craftsmen were brought to England as early as the sixteenth century but the effort was not successful.

In the course of the seventeenth century a fine English metal was developed. It was thicker than the Venetian and better suited to the taste of the English. By the eighteenth century English glassmaking had achieved a position of prominence and was admired enough to be exported.

*Traditional Glassware Transformed*

English glass was of particular importance because it became the perfect medium for designs in the light rococo style that flourished from 1730 to 1760. Engraving was particularly well suited to brilliant English products. The rococo style, whimsical in its

Goblet, with baluster stem and cover. Cover has crown and three seals impressed, 1670–1700. *The Brooklyn Museum Collection.*

Glass goblet, with a portrait of the Pretender and a two-knop air stem, circa 1710–1750. *The Brooklyn Museum Collection.*

decoration, was the first of the styles to have intimacy rather than monumentality in its best work. Designers playfully varied the classical motifs that they employed. In wineglasses the tricks of virtuosity peculiar to the glassmakers' art such as creating stripes with tubes of air in the stems were devices to lighten the necessarily heavy stem to further the allusion of lightness. When fashion changed and the more precise linear neoclassical style was introduced the glassmaker had no difficulty adjusting. Neoclassicism was a reaction against the inventiveness and whimsy of the rococo. It marked a return to employing traditional motifs as they had been known originally. It was a style for which new decorative schema were sought by going back to the art of Greece and Rome, the source of the classical style. Studying ancient sources led to a greater interest in reviving them, and to create glass faceted as it had been in ancient times resulted in an increasing popularity for cutting glass in the late eighteenth century.

*Popular Design Becomes the Source for Fine Products*

Eighteenth-century design has another side, the popular. Some of the simpler shops that had produced purely functional wares also began to meet a demand for decorative products. These were a compromise between long-standing tradition and fashion with products that are variations of high fashion analogous to country design in any of the decorative arts. On the continent these glasshouses were making simple paneled pieces decorated by crude but attractive engraving and using painted decoration that followed traditional themes associated with peasant art. The glasshouses at port towns like Bristol developed molded wares in colored glass which came closer to capturing the rococo spirit. Generally speaking the English rural scene was more affected by fashion than the rural scene on the continent.

For reasons involving economic pressures and taxation much of the English glass production of decorative wares moved to Ireland where the town of Waterford gave its name to fine cut glass before the end of the eighteenth century. The classical forms and patterns of cut glass remained in fashion through the nineteenth century. Glasshouses all over Europe made elaborate cut glass.

*Nineteenth-Century Technical Developments*

Layers of colored glass applied over clear glass and cut away to create two-colored designs, a technique introduced in the early nineteenth century, quickly came to be referred to as Bohemian glass, but it was made everywhere. This type of glass was very much in the spirit of the reaction to the Empire style which flourished from about 1830.

In glassmaking as in other fields, the nineteenth century was a period of technical innovation. There was an effort to display technical virtuosity in work that was striking and which could be appreciated by a mass audience. Old techniques like latticinio were revived. Relief sculpture on glass in a type of glass called cameo glass was introduced in the middle of the century. Paperweights were introduced in the French glasshouses as a medium for showing off the ability to work in miniature.

By the end of the nineteenth century the Art Nouveau style had come into fashion and ideas were once more as important as virtuosity.

CHAPTER IV

# American Glassmaking in the Seventeenth Century

The story of American glass begins with the very first settlements in the seventeenth century. The whole notion of manufacturing glass in an isolated colonial situation is a symptom of the philosophy of colonization in the seventeenth century. The English colonies were conceived as settlements where communities were to be founded as adjuncts to the nation rather than as simple trading outposts. In the list of logical means for making money, glass was listed as a promising industry, and the foundation of a glasshouse was undertaken in the early years.

The idea of settling a wilderness and risking starvation and attacks from savages to establish a glasshouse seems a bit ludicrous. It does seem to have happened, however, and though there is little that can assuredly be identified as the local glass made in Virginia in 1609, there is good evidence to show that the effort was made.

Virginia was settled by a joint stock company as an investment. The capital for the venture came from adventurers who remained in England and planters who went to the New World. The colony was to be financed by the company with the planters' expenses underwritten for the first years. There were many difficulties to be overcome and a lot of experimentation to be done to find the best method of conducting the business of the colony. As things worked out there was an emphasis on the agricultural activities, and the manufacturing that was started in the seventeenth century did not continue for long.

*The English
Background*

To find why anyone thought it was a good idea to manufacture glass in Virginia takes looking into the state of glass manufacturing at the time. English glassmaking in 1600 was primarily involved in making the simple utilitarian wares that had become a part of the traditional necessities known from ancient times. Although the center of the industry was in Chiddingfold, Surrey, glasshouses were dotted over England. They made simple coarse glass for windows, bottles, and other domestic forms. The objective in the glassmaking was to produce hardy metal with the usual functional qualities of glass. As a hard nonvitreous substance it was a good container for liquids; being transparent it was a practical cover for windows.

*The
Introduction of
Glassmaking to
Britain*

The industry had been introduced to Britain during the Roman era and through the centuries it had become relatively stabilized as a craft that could be compared to a folk-art medium. With care and special attention to the materials, fine craftsmen can control the color and the thinness of glass and it can be a decorative medium of great style. Relaxing the effort, the color varies and the thinness is difficult to achieve so that the results are coarse but functional. For useful glass the ingredients are easy to find. Sand and a combination of potash or soda and lime or lead are the principal ingredients of glass and these are available everywhere. Once there is a desire to produce fine glass, the problem changes and the glassmaker will work out a special formula that may involve ingredients that are available from only one special source.

*The Demand
for Fine Glass
Grows*

At the end of the sixteenth century, a second phase of glassmaking began to be developed in England. This was the production of fine glass which was influenced by the wares then made in Venice. The art of fine glassmaking had grown to impressive proportions in Venice. With the Renaissance came a growing class of those who could afford fine glass as well as an interest in Italian products which followed the classical designs that were revived first in Italy. English merchants and noblemen bought quantities of Venetian glass and the glass-sellers began to work on producing a local product that could supply their needs for fine glass. This inspired the hiring of Italian workmen and Northern Europeans who knew the secret of Venetian glass, and although in the main the efforts were not successful it was in the middle of this quest for a method of making fine glass that the idea of founding a colony in Virginia came to the fore.

*The Foundation of a Glasshouse in Virginia*

Investigations of the natural resources of the Virginia area led to the discovery that the ingredients of fine glass would be readily available, a not completely accurate notion which then resulted in the hiring of glassmakers from Germany and Italy to establish a works in Jamestown. The chief difficulty in those days was transportation. Moving raw materials about was expensive. To avoid some of that expense a few decades later, the pottery industry was attracted to Staffordshire. In the case of Jamestown, Virginia, not all the ingredients were there. Some had to be imported, but a theory had been followed and the glasshouse was built.

*Early Proofs*

The record of the establishment of the glasshouse in Jamestown is to be found in a number of early accounts of the settlement. The legendary John Smith wrote in *The Proceedings and Accidents of the English Colony in America* (London, 1624) that the glasshouse was located "in the woods neare a myle from James Towne" and this site has been excavated. In the fall of 1608 "eight Dutchmen and Poles" came in the second supply (the ship with added provisions for the colony) and according to the story, on the return run of the ship there were samples of various products that would be made at Jamestown including glass. No description of what kind of glass or what forms was given.

*Difficulties at Jamestown*

The research and excavations have been confused by the fact that the original efforts of 1608 were probably ended by the difficulties encountered in the colony a short time later. It was all but wiped out. In 1621 a second group of glassblowers were brought to the colony, sponsored by subscriptions to a "Roll." Captain William Norton and a "gange" of six Italian glassworkers came to Virginia to make glass beads that were needed for trade with the Indians, table glass and bottles that were to be sent back to England for sale. Norton was soon out of the picture and his successor was George Sandys, who is better known as a poet than a glass manufacturer. The glasshouse was operated from 1621 to 1624 but there were many problems, including a massacre, to make the extent of their output questionable. Sandys was in despair in 1623 when he wrote that although the fires had been going for six weeks there was no output to be reported and he was suspicious that the workmen "would gladly make the worke appear unfeasible, that they might by that means be dismissed for England . . ." The excavations of the National Park Service uncovered a quantity of fragments that supported the records in showing the refuse and drippings of a glasshouse. However the pieces too small to indicate what had been made and all were green glass with neither clear nor colored glass uncovered. This would seem to put into question the fact that beads or the better table glass which would have required the more sophisticated talents of the Italian workmen were produced.

There is also evidence that there may have been a later glasshouse near Jamestown on the plantation of Sir William Berkeley. A glass pot made of brick with the date 1666 on one of the bricks was unearthed near Berkeley's house, and window and bottle glass may have been made there. The mound with the pot included fragments of heavy bottles, and a fragment of window glass found in the vicinity could have been locally made.

In the year the second venture failed, 1624, the charter of the Virginia company was revoked by James I, and the colony became a royal province with basic changes in philosophy. From then on the nature of the exports that were considered desirable changed to emphasize only raw materials.

*Glass Beads and Indian Trading*

Beads were a significant factor in trading with the Indians from earliest times and whether produced in the Virginia glasshouses or not, the seventeenth-century settlers used beads in their trade with the Indians. At the turn of the century a number of strings of beads were uncovered in places that would show they were used in this trade and it was natural to attribute them to the American glasshouses. Now the attributions are questioned, but considering all the evidence it may yet be possible to show that some of the beads were from the American sites.

*Early Glassmaking in New England*

In other colonies there is some evidence of glassmaking but there is no likelihood that anything but the most ordinary useful glass was made. The town records of Salem, Massachusetts, show evidence of a glasshouse being established there by 1638, since one of the men working in it was given "one acre of land, for a howse, neere to the glass house . . ." The next year more land was given to the "glass-men" and reading the records for the years follow-ing, one gets the idea that the glasshouse was strug-gling for existence. Concessions were made to the men each year with the idea that the town might be repaid if the works were successful. In 1645 there was a petition from two of the workers for the freedom to find new backing. It is hard to surmise from the records that have survived what happened, but the glasshouse was mentioned as late as about 1670 and it is likely that the factory was in operation until then. Early digging in the area has uncovered pieces of glass that are assumed to have been made in Salem. These fragments would suggest that the product was no better than most common bottle glass. Traditional tales of the factory that were re-ported in the nineteenth century describe common domestic articles as the output.

*In New York*  Another tradition was to be found in the glass-making that was undertaken in New Amsterdam. The Netherlands had a more sophisticated industry than England in the seventeenth century and had begun producing glass that was more decorative and in the fashion of Venice so that when, by 1654, a glasshouse was established in New Amsterdam there was a good chance that it was making more than the most rudimentary functional wares. The earliest name encountered is that of Johannes Smedes who received a grant of land on what was shortly to become Glassmakers Street. Early records suggest that there was more than one glassblower in New Amsterdam and that the industry was localized on that one street. One name that stands out in the records of early glassmaking in the area is that of Evert Duyckinck, who was an artist as well as a glassmaker. He painted glass as well as making it and records show that he supplied windows for some of the churches in the area. His glasshouse was managed by Jacob Melyer after 1674, and Melyers were said to have continued in the craft for several generations.

The products of the New York glasshouses are difficult to identify. Windows in churches might well survive, but the other products are not properly recognizable. Again it would take careful documentation to go with obviously early forms to make attributions.

*In Pennsylvania*  A glasshouse is mentioned in the early records of Philadelphia. It was thought to have been established in 1683, shortly after the first settlers were brought over under the auspices of William Penn. The glasshouse is not mentioned in records of Pennsylvania that date just a few years after the foundation of the works.

Seventeenth-century American glassmaking is something of a mystery because although there is written evidence of the efforts to establish glasshouses and further proof of some activity, little glass can be securely identified until there is further research in the ways of attributing glass. Coarse glass was made all over Europe and there would have been no problem in making it in the New World, but even with some idea of the ways Americans worked and designed it takes working with a concrete body of well-documented material to find out how the American approach to design in the seventeenth century was handled in the field of glass. The chemical analyses that have been undertaken so far have been fruitful in making attributions only when there is some secure group of primary material from which to work. The variations in the metal are too great in any small glasshouse for testing to see if known recipes were used and proving an attribution that way. This is a field where the connoisseur and the conservator have to work together to establish ground rules that will lead the way to rich discovery.

# CHAPTER V

# Eighteenth-Century American Blown Glass Before the Revolution

American glass of the early eighteenth century is almost as illusive as the seventeenth-century wares, but being aware of the activity in the field may lead collectors to discoveries. Despite the rapid growth of the colonies, there were fewer efforts at manufacturing than there had been in the seventeenth century. A change in England's economic philosophy brought about a concentration on the production of raw materials and prohibition of manufacturing in the colonies. This new attitude was instituted by legislation which was not taken too seriously, for it was believed that manufacturing in the colonies would be unprofitable. As for making glass, the New York glasshouse founded in the seventeenth century may have remained in operation into the eighteenth century, but no real evidence of glass manufacturing exists until 1732. That year a map of New York was published showing the Glass House Farm near the Hudson River at what is the West Thirties today. The site was used in the nineteenth century for glassmaking, but little is known of the activity of the early years.

*The First Enduring American Glass Firm*

The opening of a glasshouse in Salem County, New Jersey, in 1739 marks the beginning of a continuous tradition of American glassmaking. The factory was founded by Caspar Wistar, a prosperous Philadelphia buttonmaker who decided, with some wisdom, to expand into the new field. He bought some two thousand acres to provide the basic raw materials for glass manufacture, contracted with four glassmakers from Holland or Germany (they sailed from Rotterdam), and built glasshouses on his new site. The community he founded was a mile outside of today's Alloway, New Jersey. The name Wistarberg was possibly given some time after it passed its prime. As late as 1885, when a history of the enterprise was written, a log house from the original building complex was still standing and the oral tradition of the greatness of the enterprise was very vital.

Four men came to set up and run the glasshouse. They were to teach Caspar Wistar and his son Richard the craft, and to receive one-third of the profits, homes, and the active assistance of the Wistars to conduct the business. From Wistar's advertisements we find that window glass and bottles were the main products. In his will, Caspar Wistar left the glasshouse to his son Richard with the stipulation that he pay his younger brother, Caspar, "400 boxes of 8×10 glass, 400 of 100 boxes of 9×11, 3 dozen ½ gallon case bottles, and 6 dozen pocket bottles . . ." That decorative pieces were produced after hours or as a sideline would seem logical, but the legend of Caspar Wistar has inspired many attributions to his enterprise that were made by the nineteenth-century glassmakers active in New Jersey. The first excavations undertaken added to the confusion because they were done without sufficient discretion, and a Coca-Cola bottle might have been classified as Wistar glass had a passing hiker tossed it in the right spot. A few bottles and more recent study of the site show that Wistar was consistent in its production of coarse green glass, and offhand objects of that metal may be from the glasshouse.

Sugar bowl, possibly by Caspar Wistar, 1750. *Courtesy, Henry Francis du Pont Winterthur Museum.*

One outstanding possibility is the sugar bowl at the H. F. du Pont Winterthur Museum, and a few examples in other collections such as that at the Salem Historical Society. A seal excavated at the site is doubtless a product of the early enterprise and it is made of the coarse glass that was found in careful recent excavations. The range of the glasshouse must have been limited and although the men may well have been imaginative in their private work, it isn't likely that a different metal would be used for their off-hours work. Blown glass that reflected the skills of the craftsmen in decorative work of varying colors was a later activity of glassworkers who concentrated their workday time on the more routine bottle and window glass. The Wistar factory continued to operate until 1780. It was described by Governor William Franklin, Benjamin Franklin's son, in a report of 1768 as making "bottles, and a very coarse Green Glass for windows" and he went on to say that "not withstanding the Duty, Fine Glass can still be imported into America cheaper than it can be made here." The report was made to ease the anxieties of those in the mother country who might feel colonial manufacturers would be a

threat to English imports, but it must have been
truthful. Richard Wistar attempted to interest the
public in buying American manufactures in 1769
and later. The war probably was responsible for the
failure of the Wistar glass enterprise, because on
October 11, 1780, *The Pennsylvania Journal* carried
an advertisement offering the factory and fifteen
hundred acres adjoining it for sale.

*An Eighteenth-*
*Century New*
*York Enterprise*

Another documented factory for which little or no
glass can be shown was organized in New York in
1752 by a group who were rather ambitious. The
rough draft of their original agreement has survived.
It called for a partnership of New Yorkers, headed
by Matthew Earnest and including Samuel Bayard,
Lodewyck Bamper, and Christian Hertell, under-
writing the journey of Johan Martin Greiner of Saxe
Weimar and supplying him with the means to
operate a glasshouse. He was to work twenty years
for the group making glass and he agreed to instruct
Mr. Earnest and his partners in the art of glassmaking. There is no proof that Greiner ever arrived,
but by 1754 the glasshouse was in operation, and its
wares were advertised for sale. They consisted of
". . . all sorts of Bottles from 1 Quart to 3 Gallons
and upwards, as also a Variety of other Glass Ware
too tedious to mention . . ." What seemed tedious
in 1754 is frustrating today, however the advertisement went on to broaden the offer ". . . all Gentle-
men that want Bottles of any size with their Names
on them, or any Chymical Glasses, or any other
sort of GlassWare, by applying to said Lepper, have
them made with all Expedition." The offer should
be read in a tense, panicky high-pitched voice because there were too few responses to achieve success. The partners had two glasshouses. They had
purchased a tract of land in Orange and Ulster

counties, New York, where timber was plentiful and a glasshouse operated there, as well as on Manhattan Island. Trouble is suggested by an announcement that "All persons that have Demands on the Company of the Glass-House at New Windsor, are desired to bring in their Accounts to Lodewyck Bamper, in New York, as speedy as possible, in order to have them adjusted by the said Company . . ." In January 1756 the pewterer John Will offered ". . . a variety of Glass Ware, manufactured at the Glass-House in New Windsor." In the July 22, 1762, *New-York Gazette or Weekly Post-Boy* we find "the Glass House Out-Houses, and all the Implements belonging thereto" offered for sale. This was the Manhattan plant which was used for entertainment and as a tavern later.

The house produced bottles, but there are only a few that may logically be attributed and none for which the proof is indisputable. Possibly the wares made would have included drinking glasses and other fine pieces, but there is no evidence. Frederick Van Cortlandt's bottles for the period have been attributed to the Glass House, and they are the usual dark green bottles, very much like the English examples of the time.

One documented example mentioned in the nineteenth century cannot be located today, but from the early description would seem to be the ordinary sort of dark green wine bottle.

Had decanters and simple tableware been produced, they would have resembled the slightly later products of the Stiegel factory.

*Glassmaking Efforts in New England*

Another attempt at glassmaking occurred in 1752 in Massachusetts. In both the *Boston Weekly Newsletter* and the *New-York Gazette* news of the arrival of German glassmakers appeared with the statement that "a House proper for carrying on that Useful Manufacture will be erected at Germantown as soon as possible." These men came to join others who had arrived a few years earlier at the behest of Joseph Crellins, a Franconian, who had received permission from the General Court of Massachusetts to bring over German Protestant glassmakers in 1748. The factory was to have been built in the Berkshire Hills between Lee and Williamstown, but the effort failed. Ever optimistic, in 1750 Crellin interested another group in starting the factory near Quincy in what was then to be called Germantown where the two groups of craftsmen were soon able to begin production. By the following year, 1753, there was a warning "that for the future none will be admitted to see the new manufactory at Germantown, unless they pay at least one shilling lawful money . . ."

The glasshouse was managed by Joseph Palmer, who explained that it was making bottles for the cider being shipped to the West Indies. A fire destroyed part of the glasshouse in 1755, and it was reestablished in 1756 by Jonathan Williams who advertised bottles, jars, chemical vessels, and window glass in the Boston newspapers until about 1760. The range of wares made at the Germantown factory was probably limited to the simpler utilitarian wares. Again, there is the possibility that a limited amount of decorative work was done, but no documented examples have turned up yet.

*The Stiegel Factory*

The most impressive glassmaking venture of pre-Revolutionary days was undertaken by Henry William Stiegel of Pennsylvania. At its height he employed 130 men to make a variety of tablewares as well as bottles and window glass, but attributions to his glasshouse are difficult to make. Having become the popular hero of the area around Manheim, Pennsylvania, in the nineteenth century, Stiegel has been credited with making all the old glass found there. As the price of Stiegel glass went up at the beginning of this century, more and more glass turned up in Manheim, some in wrappings that must have smelled of sea air from recent ocean voyages. Students have now attempted to narrow down the Stiegel group to securely documented pieces, but in doing so have probably rejected authentic material. The Stiegel glass field is confusing. The various criteria that have been established, both from the point of design and chemistry, have not held up to checking. The designs are traditional rather than original and often repeat patterns known on similar glass of European origin. Among the most securely attributed examples there is enough variation in the metal to make the content of the glass less than an ideal proof of its origin.

*Stiegel's Personal History*

Henry William Stiegel migrated to Pennsylvania from Cologne in 1750 at twenty-one years of age. He had a meteoric rise from being a poor immigrant to a prosperous ironmaster in Lancaster, Pennsylvania, which involved marrying the boss's daughter. In 1763 he opened a glasshouse which concentrated on the manufacture of bottle and window glass. After a trip to England he built a second glasshouse in 1764 which was evidently not adequate to his ambitions because he built still another a few years later in 1769.

*The Range of Stiegel Products*

Between 1769 and 1774 the Stiegel enterprise produced the variety of tableware that made it so important. The work was for Americans who wanted to have stylish homes. With agents in Philadelphia, New York, Boston, and Baltimore, the distribution must have been extensive. Company account books which have been preserved at the Pennsylvania Historical Society list what was on hand in 1769 and 1770. The range is broad and includes: plain and molded decanters; tumblers of a gill to half-gallon capacity; mugs of several types; fine wineglasses; sugar boxes and covers; candlesticks and toys. In the advertisement of 1773 the use of enameled decoration and blue glass are mentioned.

Excavations of the site in 1913 by F. W. Hunter, author of the definitive work on Stiegel glass, have occasioned a certain amount of confusion. Although Hunter was cautious in all that he did, archaeological techniques in 1913 were not perfect and the wares outlined by Hunter included nineteenth-century work. Three-mold glass and paneled vases were not made in the eighteenth century, but they were found where Stiegel was making glass. Hunter did narrow the field of what was passing as Stiegel in 1913, so the contribution he made should not be underestimated. Later scholars, particularly Helen McKearin, have suggested a working group from which new studies must be launched. After reappraising the criteria, both stylistically and chemically, the group of Stiegel work will be broadened again some day.

*Influences on Stiegel's Work*

The group of pieces attributed to Stiegel are in the spirit of the glass made by smaller glasshouses in both England and on the continent, with the sources of inspiration distinguished as separate tendencies. One tendency follows in the tradition of European peasant glass which is hard to localize. The glassmakers of places as far apart as Scandinavia and Spain worked in a related tradition which is reflected in Stiegel glass. Plain or fluted tumblers with simple engraved border decoration, and enameled bottles

Group attributed to Stiegel; American, circa 1770. Enameled mug, pattern-molded bowl, and bottle. *Cincinnati Art Museum.*

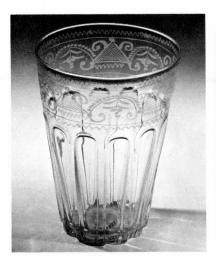 

Above Left: Tumbler with engraved decoration, attributed to Stiegel, circa 1770. *The Brooklyn Museum Collection.* Above right: Tumbler with engraved decoration attributed to Stiegel, circa 1770. *Philadelphia Museum of Art: The Charles F. Williams Collection.*

and tumblers fall into this category. In the English tradition popularly associated with the glasshouses of Bristol are the wineglasses and colored diamond-patterned molded creamers, sugar boxes, and the like. The peasant tradition was fairly consistent in design and fashion was not a factor, while in the English-style work forms and decoration reflected fashions of the time. The shape of squat globular sugar boxes was based on a rococo design also encountered in ceramics and metalwork and this shape was changed for a more classical one in later examples made after the Revolution in the Midwest. In re-establishing what was made at the Manheim factories, it is important to date what can be dated, to eliminate work done later than Stiegel operated. The wine- and jelly glasses attributed are simple and it is difficult to be sure of their origin. The fragment of an air twist stem found in Manheim raises the question of whether such work was done at Manheim.

Sugar bowl in a diamond pattern, attributed to Stiegel, circa 1770. *Philadelphia Museum of Art: The George H. Lorimer Collection.*

Tumbler and bottle with paint and enamel decoration attributed to Stiegel. *Philadelphia Museum of Art: The Charles F. Williams Collection.*

*Various Works Attributed to Stiegel*

Enameled work securely attributed to Stiegel is thought to have been limited to six opaque colors: white, yellow, blue (of a special shade), Nile green, brick red and black, applied without shading. Hunter distinguished the work of four hands, but it would be difficult to confirm his attributions. The designs include lovebirds in symmetrical patterns, floral designs, and simplified landscapes. One group with English inscriptions would most logically seem to be the work of Stiegel, but none of the group are unquestionably by Stiegel.

The tumblers vary in size and decoration. Fluted panels around the body come in different sizes and there is a generous repertory of the engraved patterns.

**American Flint Glass**

The Stiegel product was called American Flint Glass, although it did not always contain the lead that would make it flint glass. Tested chemically the results were inconsistent, varying from a soda-lime to lead glass with the former more common. Nonetheless the Stiegel works, which closed ignominiously in 1774 shortly before its entrepreneur was jailed for his debts, marked the first serious full-time effort to make finer glass in the American colonies. As securely attributed work is better understood, the group of work assigned to the Stiegel factory should be broadened.

**Stiegel's Possible Competitors**

One reason for hesitation with attributions of work that looks eighteenth-century and American, is that Stiegel glass may have had competition. In Pennsylvania newspapers of 1769 there were announcements

Mug with engraved decoration attributed to Stiegel, circa 1770. *The Metropolitan Museum of Art, New York: Gift of F. W. Hunter, 1913.*

At left: Covered mug with engraved decoration attributed to Stiegel. Attribution of the shape has been questioned, but the glass and engraving are closely connected with more positively attributed work. *The Brooklyn Museum Collection.* Top right: Pitcher possibly by Stiegel, circa 1770. Diamond pattern is typical of Stiegel. *Collection of the Philadelphia Museum of Art.* Bottom right: Expand-mold scent bottle attributed to Stiegel, circa 1770. One of many bottles related to the Manheim factory. *Philadelphia Museum of Art: The George H. Lorimer Collection.*

of a "New Glass House it is to be Hoped that all Lovers of American Manufacture will encourage . . ." The difficulties of launching a glasshouse are suggested in another series of advertisements for the Philadelphia venture. First the proprietors announced the beginning of production, but evidently there wasn't enough interest because after a lottery they then tried to be reassuring. "The Proprietors of the Glass House, near this city, having now procured a set of good workmen, and the works being in blast, the public are therefore informed that they may be supplied with most kinds of White and Green Glass Ware . . ."

The better workmen may well have come from Manheim where Stiegel was closing.

*Problems of Identification*

The production of American glasshouses has been difficult to distinguish. Simple glass is fairly consistent in design, and no matter where it is made enthusiasm of the earliest collectors lead to labeling anything crude American. Boatloads of continental and English glass were imported to fill the demand for American glass before the particular American touch was differentiated. Now, over fifty years after the first attempts to define the characteristics of American wares have been made, there are still unanswered questions. Stiegel worked in a combination of two traditions, the continental peasant and a middle-class or conservative fashionable tradition which is best seen in provincial English decorative objects of every medium. The American glass, then, includes both traditions in designs that are just a bit simpler and more direct and functional than those of Old World origin. Enameled colors are part of a simple palette and decorative motifs are boldly defined. Tumblers, with or without fluted sides, have engraved decoration that is most often not readily

Sugar bowl, in the characteristic Stiegel diamond pattern. Ohio (?), 1820. *Philadelphia Museum of Art: The George H. Lorimer Collection.*

distinguished from similar examples. In colored examples blue is all that was mentioned by Stiegel, although more variety was uncovered excavating, and bold diamond-patterned bottles, bowls, creamers, salts, and sugar boxes very close in every detail, appear in amethyst, amber, and green, too. Bold and heavy Stiegel glass at its best has qualities that are distinctively American.

# CHAPTER VI

# Nineteenth-Century American Blown Glass

The struggles for American Independence did not stop manufacturing efforts nor did victory inspire an immediate drive to step up manufacturing and make the country self-sustaining. Glassmaking continued as a somewhat difficult field for successful achievement. The range of objects that could be made from a commercial point of view was limited. Reviewing the histories of several glasshouses typical of the time will reveal the general philosophy of the industry.

*Traditional Wares*

In 1780 a number of ventures were begun, possibly because it seemed the moment to capture a market not being supplied by import. In each case, the concentration was on utilitarian wares. Bottles and window glass were offered in advertisements. The more decorative pieces, if done at all, were done less formally and for local consumption. It is customary to consider decorative ware made in limited quantities as "end of the day" work.

The Stangers established a factory at Glassboro, New Jersey, which has attracted much interest because it is thought to have continued the significant tradition of free-form blowing after the closing of the Wistar factory. At present there seems to be no

Blown candlestick. New Jersey, about 1820. *Courtesy, Henry Francis du Pont Winterthur Museum.*

real evidence of the tradition having been established by Wistar, however, although most of the traditional group of "South Jersey glass" was of nineteenth-century design.

*The Stangers of New Jersey*

The Glassboro works were established by a group of brothers named Stanger. One, at least, reported as a runaway in 1770, had been employed by Wistar. By 1784 the Stangers had been bought out and Tonkin and Carpenter operated the plant. Through many changes of management the enterprise continued into the twentieth century with bottlemaking its chief function.

The eighteenth-century decorative examples that are considered to be products of New Jersey are blown and ornamented with forms made from the molten glass. A swan finial appears on several sugar bowls. Candlesticks of simple baluster shape also have been attributed to the moment when Glassboro first prospered.

*Hewes of*
*• New England*

In 1780 Robert Hewes of Boston began building a glasshouse at Temple, New Hampshire, choosing a site where raw materials were readily available. After opening it in 1781, Hewes met with many difficulties. The first glasshouse burned down and the second fell down. There were also financial problems, and the project was abandoned. A few pieces of Temple glass which have been found are green and characteristically crude. Later Hewes was associated with the Boston Crown Glass Works. In 1782 the General Court of Massachusetts granted that company the exclusive privilege of making glass in the state for fifteen years. Before the end of the century it was making window glass in quantity and some hollow ware. Probably special

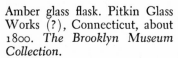

Amber glass flask. Pitkin Glass Works (?), Connecticut, about 1800. *The Brooklyn Museum Collection.*

blown pieces were made in limited quantity, too. Having been reorganized in 1809, the company expanded. A second glasshouse operated in South Boston after 1811 until the company's failure in 1827. Making fine glass, the company undoubtedly did make hollow ware for table use, although it is difficult to make attributions.

*Pitkin of Connecticut*

Another factory that began production close to 1780 was the Pitkin Glass Works at Manchester, Connecticut. It was granted a twenty-five-year state monopoly in 1783. The works were operated until about 1830 when the lack of an adequate fuel supply is thought to have been responsible for its closing.

The wares made by the Pitkins were probably in the main a variety of bottles in olive amber, amber, and olive green that were made in patterned molds and decorated with vertical and swirled ribbing. The so-called Pitkin flask which has been found consistently in the Connecticut area was made at Coventry and Keene in the nineteenth century but no proof has been found that it was made at Pitkin besides the oral tradition. The glasshouse produced bottles of every variety so that inkwells and snuff bottles are among the pieces attributed to it. Individual pieces from the same molds as the bottles include a cane, part of a cruet set, a tumbler, and a hat. One piece that can be attributed definitely is an inkwell bearing the initials JPF, for J. P. Foster, superintendent of the factory about 1810. This is straight-sided and of a deep olive amber color that is almost black.

*Lesser Houses*

Robert Morris and John Nicholson founded a glasshouse in the Philadelphia area at about the same time, 1780. It was called the Schuylkill Glass Works. Its output is not well known nor is it clear how long it operated. William Peter Eichbaum, superintendent from 1793 to 1797, is better known for his part in the Pittsburgh enterprise of O'Hara and Craig. Tablewares and window glass may have been made in the early years of the enterprise. Later, in the nineteenth century when a Schuylkill Glass Works was operated by different people, bottles were the main product. Philip Jones, active around 1810, may have used the Morris Works. But in 1813 there was Hewett, and other names were in advertisements which continue to 1823 for the local glass.

In New York State, near Albany, De Neufville, who, in spite of his name, was one of the Dutch bankers who lent money to the Revolutionary War effort, undertook to establish a glasshouse. The project was not a success. On May 12, 1785, Leonard De Neufville signed an agreement with a group to build the factory, and by 1789 the enterprise had failed. They produced window glass and bottles outside of Albany, in Dowesborough, New York. Under the name McClallen, MacGregor and Company, there was an attempt to revive work at the house in 1792, but there were moments of difficulty which resulted in a reorganization. In 1797 the Hamilton Manufacturing Society was organized to try to get the factory working once more. This continued until 1824 and crown or window glass was the mainstay of the operation. The factory may have afforded their men the opportunity of making individual blown pieces for their own use.

*Persistent Problems*

Problems were very much the same all over the country. Labor was not easy to keep and often men who teamed together to found a glass factory knew little about glass and often less about how to operate a business. Thus the possibility of success was slight.

Window and bottle glass were the ordinary products, but from these same houses came decorative work not recorded in the output because it was made for local use. The color of the decorative work was most often just whatever was used for ordinary work. and ways of ornamenting that developed seem to follow local practices that suited local taste. It is these pieces that fall into the category of folk art very easily.

*Efforts to Establish a Fine House*

An ambitious effort to make fine glass in the new Republic was begun in 1784 by John Frederick Amelung of Bremen, Germany. Amelung, backed by businessmen of his native city, established a glass factory near Frederick-town, Maryland. There they succeeded in making fine wares, the best of which were signed and dated—a unique characteristic. In a pamphlet published in 1787 as a part of the promotion, Amelung told the story of how he had founded the business. The company was formed in Bremen. The site decided upon after some investigating was near Baltimore where raw materials were readily available and encouragement might be forthcoming from the state. Amelung believed that he had not received the support he deserved either in assistance from the state or patronage by the public. His company had invested some £15,000 at the time he was writing and needed expansion. They required more enthusiastic encouragement for their enterprise, which they felt would aid the new nation. He mentioned having received recommendations from Franklin, Adams, and distinguished citizens of Maryland such as William Paca and Charles Carroll. The capital was expended on an extensive tract of twenty-one hundred acres on which they had constructed the necessary buildings for making bottle, window, and flint glass and for housing 135 "living souls." At the time he wrote, another oven was being constructed and additional men were being brought from Germany. The factory was already producing wares "of a better quality than a great deal of what is 'imported.'"

The records show that the pamphlet did produce results. Americans added some £7000 or £8000 to the original investment with Maryland lending £1000. The federal government considered contributing but did not. By not protecting glass manufacturers in the tariff acts of 1789 and 1790, it probably helped bring about the failure that caused the closing of the factory in 1795.

The output of the factory as reported in advertisements appearing in the *Maryland Journal and Baltimore Advertiser* over the years the factory was operating (1785–1795) included:

Quart, Pint, Half-Pint, Gill and Half-Gill Tumblers, wine glasses

Quart, Pint and Half-Pint Decanters, exact measure Goblet

Glass Cans, with handles of different sizes every other Sort of Table Glass

An advertisement of 1789 reported, "He also cuts Devices, Cyphers, Coats of Armes, or any other Fancy Figure in Glass." The fragments uncovered at the site show that pattern-molded pieces were made while documented examples of free-blown work reveal another aspect of the output.

The New Bremen Glass Manufactury was a large enterprise that produced a lot of glass. The documented pieces in the main are special presentation work that by the nature of their function would differ from the commercial wares, but they provide a point of departure for more serious study. It is interesting to note that although Amelung suggested that his tablewares were made of flint glass and flint glass is ordinarily defined as a lead glass, the New Bremen work of the finest quality is made of a non-lead glass that is not quite the white or colorless metal that Amelung strove for.

*Amelung's Important Work*

The important key pieces to the study of Amelung glass are dated between 1788 and 1792. The list is headed by a covered pokal with the inscription "New Bremen Glass-manufactory—1788—North America, State of Maryland . . . Old Bremen Success and the New Progress" and includes a tumbler that is inscribed: "Our very best wishes for every Glass manufactory in the United States. God Bless the City of Boston . . . Made at the Glass manufactory of New Bremen in Maryland the 23 Jan. 1789 by John Fr. Amelung & Company." The group is varied in tint. Some is faintly greenish and others a smoky color. There is handsome amethyst glass. Engraved decoration ranges from elaborate motifs with subtle variations of scrolls in heraldic designs to simple floral patterns and primitive landscapes. The use of the applied decoration on a sugar bowl for C. Geeting suggests that the technique associated with "South Jersey" was also popular at New Bremen. Amelung glass included a variety of decanters and tumblers of the simpler variety and wineglasses that are still difficult to "identify." Close checking with the key group and expanding it by careful additions of glass found in the area would make it possible to enlarge the Amelung group. At the time it was made this glass was known in more than its immediate locality, so that it doesn't have to be from a family of Frederick-town, Maryland, to be authentic, and caution is required because Amelung complained that there were Frederick-town families buying imported glass in spite of his pleas.

Clear flint beaker, presented in 1789 to John Phillips, Mayor of Boston. Amelung, New Bremen, Maryland. *Yale University Art Gallery: Mabel Brady Garvan Collection.*

Above left: Amethyst sugar bowl. New Bremen Glass Works, about 1790. A documented example for a friend of Amelung. *Courtesy, Henry Francis du Pont Winterthur Museum.* Above right: Sugar bowl with stag finial. New Bremen Glass, about 1790. *Courtesy, Henry Francis du Pont Winterthur Museum.*

Sugar bowl with stag finial. New Bremen Glass, about 1790. *Courtesy, Henry Francis du Pont Winterthur Museum.*

*Amelung's Further Endeavors*

Frederick M. Amelung's name comes up several times after the closing of the New Bremen glassworks. In 1799 he leased land at the foot of Federal Hill in Baltimore and evidently between 1800 and 1804 was involved in the operation of a glasshouse on that site. He was associated with his father-in-law, Alexander Furnival, in the undertaking. By 1805 he was off to Pittsburgh to work at the Pittsburgh Glass Works run by Colonel O'Hara. The Baltimore factory probably made some of the same wares as New Bremen, and conceivably produced bottles and window glass as staples.

*Western Glassmaking Attempts*

The question of what happened to the workmen from New Bremen has been answered by pointing to the establishment of glasshouses in the West. Amelung's appearance in Pittsburgh may have followed that of some of his workmen, and there were a number of other glasshouses that were started at the beginning of the nineteenth century.

One of the more ambitious attempts at glass-making was made by a group headed by Albert Gallatin, Secretary of the Treasury under Jefferson. It was organized as the New Geneva Glass Works in 1797 and was in production by January 1798. The active partners who knew the trade were Germans whose names recur at other houses. Later Baltzer Kramer was a partner in the glasshouse so that this glass is sometimes called Gallatin-Kramer glass. New Geneva is a town located near the Monongahela River outside Pittsburgh. According to tradition several craftsmen from New Bremen were active in the venture. The works were operated by the original group with some minor changes up to 1830. They expanded to Greensburg, Pennsylvania, about 1807. Between 1830 and 1847 B. F. Black and Company ran it until it was destroyed by fire. Window glass and bottles were the main products, but hollow glass was advertised in 1806. Bowls, decanters, glasses, tumblers, and pitchers were probably made in plain and green glass. The glasshouse had equipment to mold glass, so that ribbed examples were possible. Glass attributed to the New Geneva works are in the main fairly simple utilitarian pieces. Two goblets of unusual design, one including a medal thought to have been won by Gallatin when he graduated from the Collège de Genève in 1779, are exceptions. The securely documented examples include no work in colors other than green and clear.

Gallatin evidently realized that glassmaking was not a very profitable field. In a letter to his agent at New Geneva dated July 30, 1799, he wrote that "My present intention is either to rent or sell the Glass Works." In 1803 his business co-partnership

Blown sugar bowl. New Geneva, Pennsylvania, 1810. Attributed to a glassmaker at Gallatin's factory. *Courtesy, Henry Francis du Pont Winterthur Museum.*

Blown candlesticks. Pittsburgh, about 1810. *The Detroit Institute of Arts.*

Albert Gallatin and Company, which owned a half interest in the New Geneva Glass Works, offered it for sale by auction. The outcome of the sale is not clear because in 1816 he wrote to Matthew Lyon of Eddyville, Kentucky, in reply to a request for information on setting up a glasshouse, that he was still an investor in New Geneva. "I commenced mine with about ten thousend (sic) dollars, and made no profit during the first years nor until the capital amounted to near twenty thousand . . ." He went on to explain that the capitalization in 1816 exceeded forty thousand dollars, yet the annual profit was only about eight thousand.

Investors such as Gallatin realized much greater profits on other ventures, but he was doing what he wanted in establishing industry in the West.

*The First Pittsburgh Glasshouse*

Before the end of the century, the first of the Pittsburgh houses went into operation using coal as the fuel. Begun under the auspices of James O'Hara and Isaac Craig, businessmen who retained the services of glassmakers such as William Peter Eichbaum, Amelung, and workers from eastern glasshouses, the Pittsburgh Glass Works was opened in 1797. It was evidently not a complete success because the works were leased to Eichbaum and his partner, Frederick Wendt, until 1800. An English glassblower, William Price, was then hired to try to make flint glass but he failed. The partnership of O'Hara and Craig lasted until 1804, and O'Hara operated the works independently until 1819. In 1805 Amelung joined O'Hara, but there is little to show for his guidance. Having written to agree that Amelung should bring molds, O'Hara seemingly wanted to make pattern-molded wares. The early Pittsburgh products, like the contemporary New Geneva wares, were primarily utilitarian, and simple. O'Hara did make a variety of tableware, however, and blue was used along with clear and green, according to a 1804 document, but it was some time before the characteristic tablewares were produced.

Expand-mold compote, pitcher, and cruet. Pittsburgh, 1810–1830. *Cincinnati Art Museum.*

# CHAPTER VII

# Anonymous American Glass: Folk Art

At the factories flourishing between 1800 and the end of the century where useful wares, window glass, and bottles were the chief products, skilled craftsmen found an outlet for showing off their abilities in free-blown decorative wares and tablewares. These were made for local consumption and sometimes called "offhand" wares. Window glass and bottles were mass-produced for far-reaching markets. The free-blown material was used close to the factory, which in most cases had been set up in rural areas near a supply of fuel and other raw materials. These pieces turn up close to the sites of the early glasshouses in limited quantities, suggesting that they were a by-product rather than a major item of the glasshouses. One explanation that has been offered is that decorative work was an end of the day activity and served as gifts, but since so much is simple and useful, probably they were made more prosaically to fill the local demand for tableware. There is a theory that the special pieces were blown from particularly pure metal put aside for the job.

*Free-Blown Glass as Folk Art*

Free-blown wares have a simplicity, directness, and a traditional aspect to their design which fits within the category of folk art. The major part of the wares were of simple green or amber window glass or bottle glass, rarely colored. Forms were conceived conservatively and reflect more the exploitation of the natural qualities of glass as a medium than the fashions of the moment. The textures are most frequently the result of casual handling of the metal. Decorative elements are achieved by shaping the molten glass and adding borders and the like. The glass tends to be crude in comparison with contemporary work by sophisticated continental houses that were making tablewares, but the products of the factories are in line with timeless small-scale glasshouses that had produced functional wares for centuries. Simple pans and bowls are very much the same whether they were made in a medieval glasshouse or one of the nineteenth-century factories, and more complex shapes show their period more in overall aspects than details.

*The Sources of Free-Blown Glass*

The output of free-blown glass by the window and bottle houses is limited in range of design. Study of the work that has survived makes it appear that two distinct tendencies were followed by the glassmakers of these small glasshouses. Each tendency reflects a tradition. One stems from the Stiegel factory; the other follows the New Jersey shops that may have begun with Wistar. To define the two tendencies more fully, the Stiegel represents a combination of English and German work that was fashionable and geared essentially to middle-class taste. It is most like the contemporary efforts at Bristol and the provincial German glasshouses that were also involved with fashion. Pattern-molded glass was an important product for Stiegel and at the glasshouses that reflected his influence. The second tendency was more conservative and purely German in origin. It was less involved with the fashions of the eighteenth century and more with a traditional repertory of decorative techniques, some of which may be traced from sixteenth-century Venice, while others were the result of the ageless techniques of craftsmen producing simple glasswares. Decorative devices included applying molten glass and tooling it into patterns of various types. It also involved making looped glass, in the manner of the Venetian glass technique called latticinio, but much simpler.

Tracing the two tendencies, one finds that one was followed more in the Ohio and western Pennsylvania glasshouses while the other was followed more in the eastern houses in New Jersey, New York, and New England. Distinguishing the work of many small nineteenth-century glasshouses has begun, but it is a difficult problem since the greatest body of material can be identified only on the basis of the color of the glass and the history that has been attached to it. The fact that a piece has been discovered in a certain location is one of the determining factors in making an attribution, but a lot of work remains to be done. Chemical analysis has rarely been of much use in determining origins, since the content of a piece of simple glass generally will not be the factor to prove a specific origin for an example.

*The Problems of Free-Blown Wares*

The range in date for the blown wares covers the whole nineteenth century, but the apex of this type of work was reached before the Civil War. As production techniques improved and the glasshouses grew in size the craftsmen who could make the casual, primitive wares were replaced by more ordinary factory specialists. The smaller houses did not completely disappear until the present century, however, so it is possible to find examples that are less than fifty years old. In the field of simple blown glass there are many pitfalls. Material made in Mexico or small houses in various parts of Europe within the past thirty or forty years may be confused with the earlier American product. The small group of firmly attributed pieces must be used as the basis for establishing criteria of what is correct. The glasshouses making free-blown wares in the nineteenth century sometimes also produced blown three-mold wares which will be discussed in their own context.

*Small*
*Glasshouses*

The New Jersey glasshouses that thrived in the nineteenth century were in the main small. They concentrated on utilitarian output with bottles their most significant product. From the three or four factories active at the beginning of the century the number increased tenfold by the end of the Civil War. The glass manufacturers included some whose eighteenth-century forebears were making glass in New Jersey or Pennsylvania.

*New Jersey's*
*Characteristic*
*Products*

The New Jersey work has characteristic elements that recur in work that seems unquestionable, but at this time the characteristics of the New Jersey glasshouses are not clearly enough understood for the connoisseur to identify additional pieces turning up without pedigrees, unless they match the known ones closely.

Generally, New Jersey glass is heavy and the range of color limited. Bases of bowls and the like are made of solid crimped glass and forms are embellished by adding pieces or strips that can be tooled into patterns. One important decorative detail is the lily-pad border, which was used extensively. Another technique involved applying globs or prunts of glass to an otherwise smooth surface. These prunts were either tooled or molded. This is very reminiscent of a type of decoration used on German glass, but the metal is thicker in the New

Characteristic New Jersey pieces showing the solid crimped base and lily-pad decoration, made 1800–1850. *Cincinnati Art Museum.*

Blown sugar bowl. New Jersey, about 1800. *The Detroit Institute of Arts.*

Pitcher, blown with lily-pad decoration. New Jersey, about 1820. *Philadelphia Museum of Art: The George H. Lorimer Collection.*

Jersey version. Manipulation of the molten metal for decorative affects made it possible also to make fancy handles and to create bird finials for the tops of sugar box covers. The threads of glass were often used around the upper areas of pitchers and vases. Swirl ribbing was used by New Jersey craftsmen to create the thick lower areas of urn-shaped vases, pitchers, and sugar boxes, translating metal flutes into an appropriate pattern for glass. One important reason for the appeal of nineteenth-century glass is that the craftsmen consistently exploited their medium in ways that showed their understanding of it. Although they did not try for the finest, thinnest, and clearest glass, the thick, sometimes bubbly, slightly colored metal was handled with finesse and to advantage.

*Opaque Loops for Decoration*

A popular device for decorating the metal itself was achieved by inserting opaque colors which appeared as loops in the final product. Coming into use after 1830, looping is a technique involving skill and it was used, of course, by glassblowers in several areas besides New Jersey. The most sophisticated and delicate use of looping is to be found in sixteenth- and seventeenth-century Venetian glass, but it was used as well by French, German, and Dutch glasshouses. Closest to New Jersey work was similar work by provincial English glasshouses, that tends to be referred to as Nailsea, although it very likely was the product of other English glasshouses, too. It was made in the west, particularly Pittsburgh, and in New England. The New Jersey product is the more casual, and least refined.

*Range of New Jersey Wares*

The range of wares associated with the New Jersey glasshouses includes candlesticks, mugs, bowls, and pitchers, in shapes that reflect their times but are essentially conservative. The glasshouses that were responsible number more than forty, but for one reason or another the list of factory names encountered in the relatively few examples that have definite histories is short. The Whitney Glass Works, successors to the Stangers at Glassboro, New Jersey, the Columbia Glass Works, Fislerville Glass Works, from towns of those names, and the Eagle Glass Works of Port Elizabeth were among the factories whose craftsmen made blown glass as a sideline. They all contributed a significant chapter to the history of American glass.

Pair of vases with white loopings. New Jersey about 1850. *The Toledo Museum of Art, Toledo, Ohio. Gift of Edward Drummond Libbey.*

Above left: Blown sugar bowl. New Jersey, 1810. *Courtesy, Henry Francis du Pont Winterthur Museum.* Above center: Blown candlestick. New Jersey, about 1820. *Courtesy, Henry Francis du Pont Winterthur Museum.* Above right: Vase, a simple offhand piece. New Jersey, about 1855. *Philadelphia Museum of Art: The George H. Lorimer Collection.*

Above left: Sugar bowl. An unusual piece inscribed with its date. New Jersey, 1836. *Philadelphia Museum of Art.* Above right: Blown pitcher. Empire silver was probably the inspiration for the fluted bowl and baluster stand of this piece. New Jersey, about 1820. *The Detroit Institute of Arts.*

*New York State*   Glasshouses had been established in New York State as early as the 1750s when the Glass House Company operated two plants, one on Manhattan Island and the other at New Windsor, in a region where raw materials were more readily available. By the end of the century a glasshouse had been started near Albany and others followed near Saratoga, Watertown, and outside of Buffalo. In the course of the century some forty plants were opened. The emphasis was on window and bottle glass, but table and decorative wares were produced in small quantity. The appearance of the wares suggests the employment of New Jersey craftsmen, and this has been confirmed. Once more, decorative techniques were in a tradition that seems to derive from the European peasant models which New Jersey craftsmen followed. The glass is characteristically an aquamarine that is bright and a pale amber that tends to be warm and yellowish. Lily-pad details are favored, and generally the repertory of ornament is more limited than in New Jersey. Striped or looped work is relatively rare but does turn up. Going over the work that has survived, it would appear that more was made for use than display. The New York pieces are less fussy in detail, more graceful in line because baluster-shaped feet are often employed to lift up a bowl, pitcher, or sugar box. The lily-pad decoration tends to be tooled lightly and to swirl more than New Jersey examples. Since these differences are not always obvious, it is tempting to overemphasize them. New York glass was made in a number of glasshouses, and the best known were operating from about 1820 to 1870, as window or bottle glass manufacturers. Those that flourished near Saratoga were opened to provide containers for the mineral waters from the Saratoga spas. Congress, Saratoga, and Mountain Glass were names associated with those ventures. In other parts of the state, Redwood, Redford Crown Glass Works, Lancaster, and Lockport are significant names. The last two are known particularly for blue glass, which they made along with the more expected aquamarine and amber.

New York State glass suited a rustic taste and was the product of many craftsmen active in a variety of locations. The techniques and designs were not unique nor was there a particular desire to be original so that this type of glass is hard to trace back unless its history is known. There are consistent elements, however, which do appear evident as examples are reviewed.

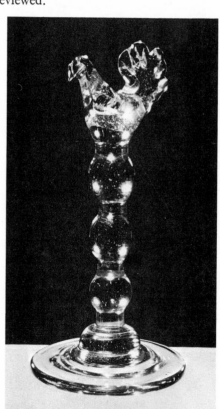

Blown "toy." Unusual offhand work. Redford Glass Works, New York, about 1850. *Courtesy, Henry Francis du Pont Winterthur Museum.*

Pitcher, blown with lily-pad decoration. New York, about 1850. *The Detroit Institute of Arts.*

Bowl and cover of dark green bottle glass. Saratoga, New York, about 1850. *The Brooklyn Museum Collection.*

*Small New England Glasshouses*

The more remote New England glasshouses produced offhand blown wares that are similar to the New Jersey and New York examples. The impetus was similar in that the factories close to fuel supplies were far from creating sophisticated wares and the craftsmen concentrating on window or bottle glass production were thankful for opportunities to be more ambitious. Since the metal used for the major

Pitcher, blown with lily pad. "Northworks" or Keene Window Glass Factory, Keene, New Hampshire, about 1850. *The Toledo Museum of Art, Toledo, Ohio. Gift of Edward Drummond Libbey.*

production items was what these craftsmen used, the colors and textures of the glass are often recognizable. The connection with New York is suggested by the popularity of lily-pad decoration.

*A Typical New England House*

Stoddard, New Hampshire, which was the scene of glassmaking from about 1840 to 1870 is a typical case. Four different glasshouses were involved, and bottles were their main product. The Granite Glass Company and New Granite Glass Company are two names found on flasks from Stoddard, but offhand blown pieces with the lily-pad decoration have been associated with the craftsmen in the town, and a reddish amber seems characteristic.

*Other Glasshouses*

The glasshouse that operated in New London, Connecticut, between about 1860 and 1870 and is known for flasks labeled Union Glass Works and New London Glass Works, was also responsible for lily-pad pieces. Aquamarine, green, and amber in several shades as well as olive glass are associated with the New London glassmakers. Many similar efforts can be found. Chelmsford, Massachusetts, Willington, Connecticut, and Burlington, Vermont, are just three more of the many towns that could boast of glasshouses where offhand wares were produced along with more commercial products.

Simple blown pieces can be identified with many different glasshouses. Wherever the tradition of a glasshouse has persisted in local legend, there is evidence in simple wares that came down as gifts or treasured family pieces, but to trace them all here is not possible. They are the by-product of craftsmen following traditional techniques they were not able to use during the working day.

Even a factory with the varied output of the Boston and Sandwich Glass Company had some offhand production. A group of banks made of clear or looped glass with strips of applied glass for decoration fall into the category. Their ovoid bodies rest on baluster stems and have tooled struts basketlike in form on which a ball and chicken finial rest. The forms were a means of showing off the skill of

Above left: Olive amber pitcher. New Hampshire, about 1820. *The Brooklyn Museum.* Above right: Pitcher, blown with lily-pad decoration by Mat Johnson. Stoddard, New Hampshire, about 1840. *The Detroit Institute of Arts.*

Above left: Blown vase. Connecticut, about 1830. *Courtesy, Henry Francis du Pont Winterthur Museum.* Above right: Molded and threaded sugar bowl. New England Glass Company, about 1820. *The Toledo Museum of Art, Toledo, Ohio. Gift of Edward Drummond Libbey.*

Pair of vases with white loopings. New Jersey, about 1850. *The Toledo Museum Institute of Arts.*

the craftsman and they date from the 1840s and 1850s.

**Western Glasshouses**

Glassmaking had been started in the west by the beginning of the nineteenth century. Factories were set up in the immediate vicinity of Pittsburgh, as well as in Ohio and West Virginia. The glasshouses were generally established to produce functional wares, particularly bottles, but a group of handsome decorative pieces have been attributed to the Midwestern houses. The most significant examples are made of pattern-molded glass in a relatively broad range of color. The diamond and fluted patterns are in a tradition related to the eighteenth-century Stiegel factory, but the shapes differ. The Midwestern forms tend to reflect the fashions of the time, are larger, and in the classical shapes of the Empire style.

Blown bank. Sandwich, Massachusetts, about 1835. *The Metropolitan Museum of Art: Gift of George Coe Graves.*

Group of expand-mold glass. Ohio, 1800–1840. *Cincinnati Art Museum.*

Expand-mold patterned bowl. Ohio, about 1830. *The Detroit Institute of Arts.*

Covered compote. Zanesville, Ohio, 1830. *The Detroit Institute of Arts.*

*Ohio's Earliest*
*Efforts*

The most famous early glassmaking effort in Ohio took place at Zanesville. In 1815 the Zanesville Manufacturing Company was organized and operated for a few years before closing. It reorganized a few times before closing again in 1838. Later it was in operation from 1842 to 1851. Flasks were the staple produced through several managements, and one company that operated the plant, J. Shepard and Company, left its mark on a few flasks of the 1820s to 1830s, while later Zanesville was inscribed on other examples. The factory was known as the White Glass Works because it attempted to make flint glass, according to early records.

Zanesville had a second glasshouse opened in 1816 and it continued intermittently until the 1840s. A marked flask from that factory bears the name "Murdock and Casell, Zanesville" to bear evidence of one of the managements.

Group of Ohio pieces, 1820–1860. The molded flask has Masonic emblems. The pitcher and bottle are simple blown pieces. The bowls in the foreground are pattern molded. *Cincinnati Art Museum.*

All in all, there were about a half dozen attempts at glassmaking in Ohio between 1820 and the 1840s, most of which did not last long. In Mantua, David Ladd and Jonathan Tinker established a glasshouse in 1821. By 1823 they had broken their partnership, but the Mantua Glass Company was in and out of business for some time after that. At Kent, then two towns known as Franklin Mills and Carthage, the same David Ladd started another factory which also closed and reopened through the next several decades. Cincinnati, Steubenville, and Ravenna were among the other locations of glasshouses in Ohio.

The blown glass attributed to Ohio includes a particularly handsome group of diamond-patterned and ribbed pieces. Bowls, salts, compotes, sugar bowls or boxes, eggs and vases are among the pieces

A selection of glass made at Mt. Clemens, Michigan, about 1850. The glass made in Michigan is in the spirit of the Ohio work. *The Detroit Institute of Arts.*

associated with Zanesville, Mantua, and Kent. Sapphire blues, amethysts, aquamarines, and ambers are the colors of these examples. The work, then, is extraordinary because it involved the use of artificial colors, or the colors not ordinarily employed for bottles and window glass. There was fine work done by the nineteenth-century glassmakers of the Midwest who followed traditional techniques which were subtly adapted to suit the taste of their day. The phenomenon of continuing eighteenth-century or age-old techniques in the nineteenth century was significant, and it has not received sufficient study to date. In many fields rural conservatism was a protection for crafts techniques that were being forgotten, and American blown glass of the nineteenth century is one good example of that.

# CHAPTER VIII

# American Cut and Engraved Glass

American cut and engraved glass has been produced in great variety of patterns and styles over the last two hundred years. Beginning with the first mention of glass cutters in about 1770, there is evidence of activity from then on. Unfortunately, it is not always possible to match examples to factories that are documented, and, particularly for the early years, very little is marked and securely attributed. Not all the patterns of American glass can be recognized now, so that it is likely that examples thought to be European will be proved American, as documented work by glass cutters from New York, Baltimore, Philadelphia, Boston, and Pittsburgh is identified.

Since a continual influx of skilled craftsmen from the Old World has been used to carry on the glass-cutting activities from before the Revolution until today, a variety of influences have affected cut-glass design. However, these influences were generally assimilated so that, in spite of changing fashions, there has been a consistent approach to design evident in American work.

*The
Glass-Cutting
Process*

Cut and engraved glass involves ornamentation achieved by grinding into a glass surface. For the best results the glass should be clear and colorless. Cut-glass design most frequently has been of classical inspiration with many changes through the years, the result of technical improvements. The glass metal was purified constantly and the mechanics of cutting were simplified to allow for more complex patterns. As technical abilities improved, a good deal of cut glass was made to show off the virtuosity of the craftsman, but there are examples in which engraving is more significant than the cutting.

*Major Styles of Cut Glass*

The history of American cut glass can be divided into four styles. First is a combination of rococo and neoclassical: light in scale with small patterns on shapes reflecting both styles, although gradually the Greco-Roman forms typical of the neoclassical predominated. This flourished from about 1770 and 1820. The second is heavier in scale and more elaborately cut. It is characteristically in the spirit of the Empire style. The style flourished until about 1840 when new influences reflecting continental glass fashion resulted in less elaborately cut pieces and experiments with colored glass. The style is one facet of the rococo and Renaissance revivals that were flourishing and that persisted until after the Philadelphia Centennial in 1876. The fourth style marked the period of great virtuosity when glass cutting had reached a new height of refinement through the use of new sands and new fuel and electric power was introduced to run the wheel lathes for cutting glass. This made it possible to achieve the great intricacy responsible for the period being popularly called "Brilliant" which thrived until the '20s when interest lagged. Since then some interesting engraved work has been undertaken but it is hard to make general appraisals.

*The Nation's First Glass Cutters*

Probably the first mention of a glass cutter in America is Stiegel's request for one in an advertisement of June 20, 1771, in *The Pennsylvania Journal and Weekly Advertiser*. There he said, "A glass cutter and flowerer, on application will meet with encouragement . . ." According to his account books, Stiegel employed several glass cutters. The contract of one of them, Lazarus Isaacs, dated 1773, has survived. Isaacs had advertised earlier in 1773 that he cut and engraved "on glass of every kind in any figure whatsoever . . . ," explaining that he had just come from London. The Stiegel work involved little cutting but more engraving. Isaacs was probably responsible for some of the surviving work. Forms were often traditional and the decoration was light-in-scale peasant motifs as often as distinctively rococo.

*The Early Neoclassical Style*

The Amelung enterprise at Frederick, Maryland, and the Baltimore factory that succeeded it, were responsible for simply cut and elaborately engraved pieces. Both glasshouses are associated with light, delicate work. Although some forms were occasionally very conservative in shape and presentation pieces repeat earlier eighteenth-century designs in their heavy baluster stems and general outline, the decanters are simple but obviously neoclassical. Table glasses were also in the fashion of the time. This neoclassical style in glass involved the use of garlands of small flowers, stars, as well as other more abstract motifs in the same delicate feeling. Shapes were also simple and light and the glass was thin.

*The Empire Style—Later Neoclassical*

The Empire style, introduced on the American scene as early as 1810, is a second phase of the neoclassical. Both heavier in proportion and more dependent upon ancient Greco-Roman models, Empire-style cut glass faintly echoes faceted Roman glass. The newer product was designed to show off the craftsman's abilities and the brilliance of the metal so that cutting tended to achieve deeper

Above left: Pitcher with engraved decoration. Pittsburgh, 1810. *Courtesy, Henry Francis du Pont Winterthur Museum.* Above right: Sugar bowl with engraved decoration. Pittsburgh, about 1810. Early engraving typical of the Pittsburgh area. *The Metropolitan Museum of Art, New York.*

Cut and engraved vase. Pittsburgh (?), 1820. *The Brooklyn Museum Collection.*

Decanter and glasses of cut and engraved glass. Pittsburgh, 1817. Thought to have been made for James Monroe. *The White House Collection: Photograph from the Smithsonian Institution.*

Wineglass. This cut-glass strawberry and diamond pattern was popular in Pittsburgh although also known elsewhere. Pittsburgh, about 1830. *The Brooklyn Museum Collection.*

ridges that were more highly reflective than ancient examples. The glass was fine enough to be clear, colorless, and without bubbles or other imperfections even though it was thicker. The shapes that were of greatest appeal were squat and heavy. Pittsburgh is a center of glassmaking that came into particular prominence in the period after 1810. One company that has become associated with fine cut glass to the degree that almost anything made between 1820 and 1850 is attributed to them is Bakewell's, known first as Bakewell and Ensell, then B. Bakewell and Company, and later as Bakewell and Page. The efforts of the company, founded in 1808, were generously lauded for a good part of its career. President Monroe purchased a large set of tablewares from the firm in 1817. Some of this is engraved with the Arms of the United States, and other pieces have floral ornamentation. These are in the squat shapes of the Empire style. An early

Above left: Cut-glass decanters. Pittsburgh, about 1810. A gift from Albert Gallatin to a member of the du Pont family. *Courtesy, Henry Francis du Pont Winterthur Museum.* Above right: Cut-glass tumbler. Pittsburgh, about 1820. *Courtesy, Henry Francis du Pont Winterthur Museum.*

description says that they were cut by Jardelle, a French craftsman. The pattern that is most readily associated with Bakewell's early work won them an award at the Franklin Institute of Philadelphia in 1825. It is called strawberry diamond and fan.

*Problems of*    Problems in attribution become apparent when one
*Definite*      considers The Union Flint Glass Company of
*Attribution*    Philadelphia. The firm operated from 1826 to 1844, employed one hundred hands and had two warehouses. They must have made quantities of glass. We know that they made pressed glass as well as cut glass. The work was described by contemporaries as very fine. In 1827 the Franklin Institute exhibited specimens of their glass but today any work attributed to the factory can only be tentative.

*The New*
*England Glass*
*Company*

The New England Glass Company, founded in 1818 and much more famous for molded wares, produced important cut glass. In an advertisement of April 15, 1818, in *The Boston Commercial Gazette* is the announcement that "They have now on hand at the Manufactory, a complete assortment of FLINT GLASS of superior quality," and also:

> "Attached to their Manufactory they have an Establishment for *Cutting Glass* in all its variety operated by Steam Power, and conducted by experienced European Glass Cutters of the first character for workmanship in their profession."

> "Any article made or cut to pattern, or particular direction, at the shortest notice."

By 1823 the firm employed 140 workmen and their yearly sales were $150,000. In 1825 a cut-glass bowl by the New England Glass Company was shown at the Washington exhibition of manufactures, and later at its 1827 exhibition a silver medal was awarded to the company by the Franklin Institute.

The factory grew steadily and by 1849 there were 450 employees. It would seem logical that the output was similar to Bakewell's and as varied, with some distinctive pattern favored over the strawberry diamond and fan.

*New York*
*Glass*
*Companies*

In 1820 the New York Glass Company was founded to make flint glass and they, too, more than likely were responsible for fine work. The firm's main stockholders, the Fisher Brothers and John Gilliland, split after a few years with Gilliland establishing the Brooklyn Glass Company in 1823. Both companies and Jackson and Daggott, which had started in 1819 as a glass-cutting establishment, were active on the New York scene, and although the first was soon forgotten, this group was the core of a thriving local industry whose shops are now hard to link to existing glass.

*High Quality of the American Product*

All cut and engraved glass, wherever it was made, followed the same basic concept that the deeper the cutting the richer it looked. Obvious parallels with English and Irish work can be made and until more is known it will be difficult to distinguish the various American trends. The extent of flint glass made in the United States was described in a federal report by the Committee on Glass and Manufactures of Clay which put the total product of flint glass at $1,300,000, ". . . of which $400,000 was made in two of the largest [glasshouses] at Boston, much of the latter consisting of cut glass . . . Few if any orders were sent abroad for flint glass by American merchants . . ."

The 1831 account is quoted by J. L. Bishop in *History of American Manufactures* which gives another account of American glass a bit later:

The American Flint Glass rivalled in solidity and elegance that of foreign countries. The Glass manufacture altogether, including window glass, glass bottles, etc. employed three thousand and two hundred and thirtysix persons in eightyone glass houses and thirtyfour glass-cutting establishments in which was produced a value of nearly three million dollars . . . The manufacture of flint glass which from 1824 to 1836 had rapidly increased, and in 1842 employed seventeen furnaces had gradually declined with the reduction of duty . . .

That is to say that by the middle of the nineteenth century there were problems confronting glass manufacturers which may have been very involved.

*New Sources
for Glass
Design*

There were innovations in glass design in the 1840s. These were simply manifestations of changes in the arts that had begun a little earlier. The most simple explanation is that the changes were a reaction to the classical which had dominated. In the early decades of the nineteenth century, ancient Greece and Rome were the major sources of inspiration. Then the sources broadened to suit the changes in taste. Eighteenth-century French rococo design, the sixteenth-century Renaissance, and the seventeenth-century Baroque all served as the basis for nineteenth-century designs, which were careful adaptations of the original styles to suit the later needs. The whimsical rococo became the most popular of the styles revived in the nineteenth century, but it was less suitable for cut glass than for ceramics and metalwork. Nonetheless, the rococo is reflected in the smaller scale of characteristic shapes and the lighter feeling of decorative details. The use of color and of new flatter types of cutting are especially significant.

The period between 1840 and 1876 is one which saw the continuation of the more successful glasshouses formed earlier. A crucial test of stability had come with the financial chaos of 1837, but in Pittsburgh, Boston, and New York the more famous of the flint-glass manufacturers and cutters were able to continue to flourish.

*New Concepts
in Glass
Decoration*

As the technical abilities of manufacturers improved, new kinds of decoration were developed. On the continent, the use of color in combination with clear glass was introduced. The new type was called Bohemian glass and imports were offered early by the dealers in the larger American cities. The technique, involving applying layers of colored glass over the clear and cutting and engraving panels or dec-

Above left: Ruby-glass wineglass with engraved decoration by Louis Vaupel. The New England Glass Company, about 1860. *The Brooklyn Museum Collection.* Above right: Cologne bottle with engraved decoration. The New England Glass Company, about 1860. *The Brooklyn Museum Collection.*

oration, was one which depended upon the contrast of clear and colored glass for effect rather than extensive and intricate relief. This resulted in forms that were quite different from the earlier examples. There is a connection between Bohemian glass and the rococo revival style in floral ornaments and scale. A secondary style of the period, the Renaissance revival, is even more closely related since the forms and details of the panels of the Bohemian-type echo sixteenth-century motifs just as did Renaissance revival furniture. The bigger factories were all capable of doing Bohemian-type glass, but few pieces have been identified with American sources other than documented work from Boston and Sandwich and the New England Glass Company.

Cut-glass compote. The New England Glass Company, about 1870. *The Brooklyn Museum Collection.*

Where technical prowess in laying color on clear glass is so important and when decorative details are fairly routine, it becomes difficult to work out characteristics that are surely American. The general standards of simplicity and straightforwardness may be applied to a phenomenon as elaborate as this type of glass, but assembling a larger group is necessary before many pieces with American histories can be attributed to the local manufacturers. In the nineteenth century glass imports were significant, but, unfortunately, since it was more fashionable to have the import than a local product, the advertisements of the period tended perhaps to overemphasize the availability of foreign wares. Statistics show that the American glasshouses employed many people and must have produced extensive amounts of glass.

*Clear Glass*      In the more significant clear glass of the period, a desire for simplicity often resulted in limited cut areas, and a more extensive use of engraved decoration. One manufacturer who set up his glasshouse in this period was Christian Dorflinger, who operated in Brooklyn between 1852 and 1863, then after a short time was re-established at White Mills, Pennsylvania. The quality of Dorflinger glass has always attracted admiration so that if a piece fits into the time Dorflinger was in business, the temptation is to attribute fine work to his glasshouse. The work of the early period shows fine cutting used on forms that were light in feeling. Engraved decoration used without cutting faceted panels is encountered on groups of delicate early Dorflinger work. The forms of decanters reveal this same tendency to lightness and the rococo.

Cut-glass vase by Christian Dorflinger. (Long Island Flint Works), 1859. *The Brooklyn Museum Collection.*

Cut-glass decanter and glasses by Christian Dorflinger. (Wayne County Glass Works), 1876. *Philadelphia Museum of Art: The George H. Lorimer Collection.*

Dorflinger's fine quality is confirmed by the important orders he received. Dorflinger glass was used in the White House by the Lincolns. It is typical of its day as far as general ornament goes.

*Inferior Products*

One element of confusion in the history of cut glass is the result of competition in the post-Civil War period. Lime glass had been developed as a cheap substitute for flint glass. First used in 1864, it was not hard enough to be a good medium for cutting. Cut glass made of it tends to be fuzzy because it wears easily. Cut lime glass was made fairly late in spite of the disadvantages, because it could be sold quickly to those not concerned with detail. This kind of deception, while not unusual in the nineteenth century, is actually more typical of twen-

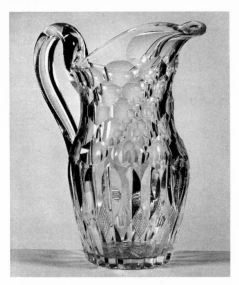

Cut-glass pitcher by Christian Dorflinger. (Wayne County Glass Works), about 1875. *The Brooklyn Museum Collection.*

tieth-century "knock-offs"—copies made with details of one sort or another omitted to cut costs. The "knock-off" in cut glass was made on a molded rather than blown-glass blank and often the mold marks get in the way of the design. Unlike many other substitutes where a new esthetic developed out of cheapening and popularizing decorative objects, no compromises were made to create designs that would exploit the qualities of lime glass.

*The "Brilliant" Period*

The most flamboyant cut glass was made in the Brilliant period dating from 1880 to 1929. The first obvious signs of the change in taste and approach can be seen in the glass exhibited at the Philadelphia Centennial in 1876 where the New England Glass Company showed a variety of deeply cut pieces in shapes that were inspired by several historical styles. The end of the period may be discerned by changes in taste that took place in the 1920s and by the Depression which followed when luxurious cut glass became extraneous.

Cut-glass goblet. The New England Glass Company, about 1875. *The Brooklyn Museum.*

*Signs of Progress*

Cut glass was a special phase of the glass industry that was not important insofar as total production goes, but it was profitable and it did show the quality of glass manufacture. There were other signs by the 1880s of how far the industry had progressed. In 1883 the U. S. Government Printing Office published a report on glass manufacturing in Europe to serve as a guide for American manufacturers who wanted to export. It is amusing to read that the reasons listed for the failure of glass exports were delivery problems and design rather than cost and quality. According to the report, Americans preferred shapes that did not appeal to Europeans. By 1902, eighty cutting shops employing thirty-five hundred cutters were said to be operating in the United States, and although designs were frequently patented, unmarked pieces are not easy to identify.

The glasshouses involved in producing elaborate

cut glass either specialized in fine tablewares or made bottle and window glass, too. In any case, the houses were distributed over the country with concentration in areas where fuel, raw materials, or shipping was convenient.

*"Brilliant"*
*Characteristics*

Brilliant cut glass characteristically has relatively deep faceting in overall patterns. Much of the decorative cutting is in the diamond patterns popular in the 1820s but deepened to appeal to later taste. The technical innovations that made it possible to make the deeper cuts were the development of a purer glass metal through the use of gas heat and the introduction of new equipment for brushing and cutting.

There are quite a few patterns in Brilliant cut glass. Some were used by a variety of glasshouses while others were exclusive to the houses that introduced them. The use of a pattern, even if patented as the identifying detail, is not always safe, but there are a group of glasshouses that dominated the field and may serve as a point of departure for making attributions. The best-known glasshouses of the period can be used to show the work that is typical.

*The Prominent*
*Houses*

*C. Dorflinger and Sons*, White Mills, Pennsylvania, made glass of the Brilliant period which was often thinner than competitive work and they used colored glass more. *Libbey Glass Company*, Toledo, Ohio, originally the New England Glass Company, had moved west in 1888. This put them closer to new sources of fuel and enabled the management to reorganize. Its exhibition at the Columbian Exposition of 1893 in Chicago presented elaborate American glass at its finest. *Gillinder and Sons*, working first in Philadelphia where they were known for pressed glass made for the Centennial, made fine cut glass in Greensburg, Pennsylvania, from 1883 on. The work was conservative in pattern and of a fine metal. The *Pairpoint Glass Company,* called Pairpoint Corporation, is also known for conservative design. Floral motifs were frequently engraved on flat areas. In many instances, designs were updated by the addition of stars, fans, or extra lines. *T. G. Hawkes Glass Company* opened in Corning, New York, in 1880 and has always made particularly fine work. Primarily a cutting shop, Hawkes owned Steuben Glass from 1903 to 1918 and blanks were supplied by the subsidiary but were blown to Hawkes' specifications. At first, Corning had supplied the blanks, and after Steuben was taken over by Corning Tiffin Glass was a prime source of blanks. Hawkes is distinctive in exploiting new patterns that are rich without being overly flamboyant, but they did work as fine as any done in Brilliant cut glass.

Cut-glass finger bowl by Christian Dorflinger (Wayne County Glass Works), 1897. *The Brooklyn Museum Collection.*

Naming five of the eighty shops that were recognized by William Dorflinger in a speech he made in 1902 is hardly giving the complete story. It suggests the scope, however, and serves to remind students of the vast amount of work to be done in studying this phase of glass.

*"Brilliant"*
*Design*

Cut-glass design of the Brilliant period is varied. Since brilliance is achieved by creating a faceted surface, the patterns were devised in attempts to create as reflective a surface as possible. One tendency was conservative and simply reused popular early patterns in higher relief. New designs were based on fresh combinations of reflective motifs. Crosshatching, waffle patterns, diamond-like faceted forms, and stars were among the motifs put to use in infinite variations and combinations. The waffle grid was occasionally distorted into an expanded diamond pattern and filled with stars and crosshatches alternately. Canework is sometimes recalled by the motifs, and designs vary from tight symmetry to very free, almost asymmetrical patterns. After 1910 there was a growing tendency toward leaving small areas of the surface plain. Large flowers came into favor and in lesser work the basic patterns of the '90s were enlarged in scale to provide the plain areas with heightened contrasts.

Considering the technical feats, the late cut glass is remarkable; and notwithstanding the great amount of highly repetitious and unoriginal design, there were important examples of the period that are distinctive documents in the history of the decorative arts of the period.

# CHAPTER IX

# Molded Glass

As might be expected, nineteenth-century changes in approach led to mass-produced molded glass by about 1820. Molds had been used much earlier, but between about 1810 and 1820 the use of a three-piece full-size mold to make the patterned glass, called blown three-mold, was introduced. The development may have been American, but evidence is insufficient to determine its origin. The simple molded patterns are similar to English and Irish products roughly contemporary with them, and which came first cannot be determined. One hypothesis is that Thomas Cains, an English glassmaker who made flint glass in Boston from 1812 on, introduced the blown three-mold glass. The partisans of that idea are split on whether he had learned about molds before he migrated or invented the mold to cope with the competition from England. Whichever is true, and whoever was responsible for introducing the new technique, it was not extensively used before 1820. About the only evidence of any molded glass being manufactured before 1820 is the 1819 advertisement of the New·England Glass Company which mentions "Prest Castor Bottles" and "moulded half" bottles. The 1820 advertisement includes plain and molded decanters with ball and "prest" star stoppers as well as molded and plain tumblers. There is no final proof that the references mean blown three-mold, but the designs are timely for that moment.

The use of the full-size mold becomes more puzzling because the technique was displaced by mold-pressing glass which followed very shortly. Both types of molding produced relief-decorated glass that relates to cut glass and serves as an inexpensive substitute for it. Both have attracted interest and admiration because they have been developed with an understanding of the limitations of the process involved.

*Blown Three-Mold Glass*

Blown three-mold glass is characterized by relatively flat over-all relief decoration in a variety of patterns. In most cases the pattern is seen in reverse on the inside of a piece and marks of the mold are evident. The repertory of motives is extensive and all were used in creating over-all patterns based on cut glass of the period between 1820 and 1840.

Research on designs of the molds and where they were used has led to some attributions of this type of glass. Oddly enough, although this type was known as Stoddard glass at the beginning of the century, it seems certain that blown three-mold glass was never made at Stoddard, New Hampshire, where it was once thought to have originated. The patterns that can be securely attributed to date are a fairly small part of all that are known.

*New England Activities*

The New England Glass Company made small salts which their 1820 advertisement described as "fan-end and octagon." These have sides in a rib and diamond pattern, are thick and are part of a group of molded pieces that may be called "Imitation Cut Glass," but which relate to the three-mold pieces probably made a short time later. The New England company has been credited with blown three-mold pieces in patterns of Gothic arches and cornucopias.

The Boston and Sandwich Glass Company was active in the production of three-mold glass before 1850. Fragments found on the site of the factory confirmed the long-standing tradition of their extensive activity in this field. The designs attributed

Blown three-mold perfume bottle, fluted pattern. Probably Boston and Sandwich Glass Company, about 1820. *The Brooklyn Museum Collection*

Early pressed-glass mold salt. The New England Glass Company, about 1820. A type contemporary with the introduction of blown three-mold. *The Brooklyn Museum Collection.*

Blown three-mold vase in sunburst pattern; blown three-mold pitcher in horizontal palm-leaf pattern; blown three-mold tumbler in diamond and fluting pattern. Boston and Sandwich Glass Company, about 1820–1830. *Cincinnati Art Museum.*

Above left: Blown three-mold decanter, blue glass. The New England Glass Company, 1820–1830. "Baroque" pattern. *Philadelphia Museum of Art.* Above right: Blown three-mold decanter (marked Rum). American, 1820–1830. *Courtesy, Henry Francis du Pont Winterthur Museum.*

to Sandwich include several types of spiral-ribbed toilet bottles, a variety of straight-ribbed pieces, diamond-diapered glasses and a number of examples of the sunburst motif. There were blue and yellow pieces along with the clear to prove that Sandwich used color. The range of design was broad. Besides those that are most easily categorized as Empire style, there were examples with the pointed arch motif that is easily equated with the Gothic revival and scroll patterns that have been called Baroque, and are actually a part of the rococo revival of that period. This molded glass was made in a variety of pieces, including decanters, glasses, bottles for cologne, castor sets and the like, tumblers, and pitchers.

Above left: Blown three-mold preserve dish and plate. Possibly Boston and Sandwich Glass Company, about 1820. *The Henry Francis du Pont Winterthur Museum*. Above right: Blown three-mold mug, blue glass. American, about 1820. *The Brooklyn Museum Collection*.

At Coventry, Connecticut, a glasshouse which operated from 1813 to 1848 produced three-mold work. The output of this house included tumblers, decanters, canisters, flasks, bottles, and inkstands. Olive amber was a popular color at this establishment for molded glass as well as bottles.

Another site of some importance was the Marlboro Street Factory at Keene, New Hampshire. Colorless flint glass was used along with the more usual green bottle glass for the blown three-mold pieces made at Keene. The forms included decanters and inkwells with variations such as tumblers seeming to be of handwork. The patterns associated with Keene are various diamond and rib and sunburst designs. The group of New England glasshouses for which securely attributed work is known is still limited. Considering the variety of the character of the houses the type was probably much more widely made.

*New York Companies*

In New York the Mount Vernon Glass Company is the only well-documented maker of blown three-mold glass. A heavy, grossly ribbed decanter is characteristic of the glasshouse with dark green and aquamarine colors frequently encountered. The same gross handling of detail is found on a decanter in the sunburst pattern attributed to Mount Vernon. The letterhead of James Gilliland and a few of the other New York houses mentioned plain, molded, and cut glass so that one wonders if perhaps the glasshouses in New York City and Brooklyn also made this kind of glass.

*The Western Evidence*

The New Jersey and Pennsylvania houses have not turned up any quantity of blown three-mold, but the Ohio sites which have been properly excavated do show that the glass was made there. In both Mantua and Kent, Ohio, bottles, bowls, decanters, and pitchers have been found in patterns that appear to have been local. In excavations of the sites, blown three-mold fragments have turned up in quantity.

Blown three-mold glass in geometric patterns. Left to right: Decanter in sunburst pattern by Mt. Vernon Glass Works; bowl from Kent, Ohio; decanter in bold pattern by Mt. Vernon Glass Works. *The Brooklyn Museum Collection.*

Blown three-mold bottle in spiral fluted pattern. Probably made in Ohio, about 1840. *The Brooklyn Museum Collection.*

*The Uses of Blown Three-Mold Glass*

Blown three-mold glass is very special in its flat over-all patterns. Although only a few of the many molds used have been associated with specific glass-houses it is fairly safe to assume this type of glass was made in different parts of the country as a common inexpensive tableware. It met the need for a type of glass that would be competitive in a market that might otherwise have been flooded with imports. From all indications the molds simplified the process of making fine wares to a degree that made production fast without radically changing the shop setup so that for a house making bottles, taking on the blown three-mold was no problem. Esthetically the new type fits into the large group of objects made before 1850, which reveal a compromise between fashion and function. For the middle-class man knowing he would not be able to afford the more elaborate cut glass, this very frank adaptation seemed to be appealing. It could never be confused with cut glass because the feeling and appearance are so different. At the same time, there are striking similarities in shapes and the vibrant surfaces. The relation between molded glass and cut glass is analogous to connections between high-style, elegant furniture and the simple painted work of the same time. In each case the less elegant product is conceived consistently and successfully.

# CHAPTER X

# Pressed Glass

Pressed glass is a step further from blown glass than molded, and is a second important phase in the nineteenth-century developments of the American glass industry. Involving the use of a mold in which the glass gather was literally pressed with a plunger, this new type of glass required skilled mechanical handling but less craftsmanship than the earlier techniques that required the services of a glassblower. The artistry was passed from the man working the molten metal to the designer of the mold. The new technique inspired new esthetics, and over-all patterns which were begun in imitation of cut glass were soon created in textures peculiar to the new process.

To avoid large smooth areas that might be unattractive, and when decorative swirls were absent, stippling was applied. The glass was called Lacy because of the lacelike affect achieved with the over-all patterns.

*History of Pressed Glass* — Pressed glass had been made in the late eighteenth century in England and the Netherlands. It was used for small pieces and for the feet and bases of larger work. The American development was distinctive and regarded as something of an innovation. Apsley Pellatt, an English manufacturer, in his book *Curiosities of Glass Making* (London, 1849) said, "the invention of pressing glass by machine has been introduced in England from the United States of America . . ." Strangely enough one of the men who was responsible for the introduction of pressed glass, Deming Jarves, who had been associated with both the New England Glass Company and the Boston and Sandwich Glass Company and was awarded one of the early patents for pressing glass, questioned the statement. In his *Reminiscences of Glass-Making* (New York, 1865) he said, "Although it is commonly believed here that the invention originated in this country, the claim cannot be fully sustained . . . [but] America can claim the credit of great improvements in the needful machinery which has advanced the art to its present perfection . . ."

Just when the process had been developed to the point of working smoothly is also open to question. Simple pieces were being made in the late 1820s. The patent records of the early 1820s have been destroyed, so we know only of the succession beginning in 1825 with Bakewell's for a furniture knob. There were a number after that, mostly for furniture knobs and one of 1827 to Phineas Dummer of the Jersey Glass Works for a "cover plate." Deming Jarves received a patent in 1830 for a mold that would include a handle on a hollow piece made by pressing. This may be considered a final step in the maturation of pressed glass, although there were many later improvements. At any rate, the technique was introduced in the 1820s and improved with increases in quality and quantity after 1830. It was used by a number of glasshouses and work of the Lacy type was made until about 1850.

*Lacy Glass*

Molds for Lacy glass were complex and expensive to make. It is thought that in about 1840 a change in taste accompanied by a desire on the part of the manufacturers to make simpler and less expensive molds brought the Lacy period to an end.

Early clear pressed-glass salt. The New England Glass Company, circa 1827. *The Brooklyn Museum Collection.*

Lacy glass was traditionally attributed to the Boston and Sandwich Glass Company without regard for the few marked examples that pointed to other houses as possibly responsible. The story has been clarified to some degree and about sixteen factories are known to have made pressed glass before 1850.

*The Earliest Efforts*

The earliest pressed glass was simple and heavy. Designs were inspired by cut glass with occasionally exceptional details in relief such as the sheaf of wheat, the profile of a hero, the lyre. Technically, there was a problem in controlling the flow of glass into the mold so that results were not consistent, but this adds to the appearance since the forms are generally primitively conceived. Furniture knobs, cup plates and salts of the period before 1830 have been identified. The salts are most interesting and one form encountered is that of a plain, rectangular-based, open box with columns at the corners, and relief ornament applied to the sides. These have been found with the marks of the New England Glass Company and the Jersey Glass Company.

*The Spread of Pressed Glass*

The pressed glass that is more characteristic was made after 1830 and began to go out of style in 1840. Typical are delicate designs which are complex and ornate. The motifs are derived from a broad vocab-

ulary of ornament, mostly classical but including
rococo and Gothic details in over-all patterns with
the background often stippled, lined, or roughened
in some way. The surface of pressed glass is made
highly reflective by the faceting. The glass itself is
dull-looking mat finish rather than glossy so that all
the light and brilliance of pressed glass is due to
the relief ornamentation. Pressed glass between
1830 and 1840 most often was decorated with a
low-relief over-all pattern that was delicate but
sharply defined. The scale and general effect no matter what the style of the ornament was closely related to the rococo revival style which was beginning to appear in all the decorative arts.

*Regional
Distinctions
Among Pressed-
Glass Houses*

The glasshouses that made pressed glass were located
in each of the significant glassmaking districts, but
the distinguishing characteristics of each area may
be difficult to determine. The New England houses
were in the main the most sophisticated. New England Glass and the Boston and Sandwich Glass
were the companies responsible for the finest work,
presumably. Two other glasshouses, Mount Wash-

Pressed-glass sugar bowl with
cover. Boston and Sandwich
Glass Company, 1840–1850.
*The Toledo Museum of Art,
Toledo, Ohio.*

ington Glass in South Boston and Providence Flint Glass, Providence, Rhode Island, were making pressed glass, but very little is known of their output. The New England designs are thought to be the most cohesive and the most elaborate. They tend to combine the greatest number of motifs possible with obvious skill. The forms include cup plates, salts, and a variety of larger pieces such as compotes, platters, covered sugar bowls, and lamps.

*Pressed-Glass Design*

As far as design goes, although the early work evidently is derived from cut-glass models, the emphasis of the period is on a new approach, with a large repertory of small motifs employed in over-all designs. Sometimes the sources of pressed-glass designs are found in decorative porcelains of the period with the painted decoration translated to relief ornamentation. In these cases it seems as though the designer reads the surface of a pressed-glass piece as a flat surface with the decoration linear ornament. The range is too broad to account for all the specific designs; however, there was a consistency in all the work.

Although several New York and New Jersey glasshouses are known to have made pressed glass, and in 1831 Gilliland of the Brooklyn Flint Glass Company won an award for pressed glass at an American Institute Fair, no documented pieces have been discovered. Probably work from these houses has been attributed to Sandwich.

*Midwestern Pressed Glass*

The Midwestern houses, those of western Pennsylvania and West Virginia, namely Bakewell and Company, the Fort Pitt Glass Works, the Stourbridge Flint Glass Works, the Union Glass Works, the Birmingham Flint Glass Company, and the Pennsylvania Flint Glass Works, all of Pittsburgh,

Pressed-glass cup plates. Boston and Sandwich Glass Company, 1830–1850. *Collection of the Philadelphia Museum of Art.*

and Ritchie and Wheat, and Wheeling Flint Glass of Wheeling, West Virginia, worked in a different style. Their designs were more stiff and less sophisticated. There is a primitive quality that makes them recognizable and adds a special charm. The designs tend to relate closely to the models made at Sandwich, but the parts don't fit together as well.

*Uses of Lacy Glass*

Lacy pressed glass was used for many different kinds of objects, but not sets of glasses. It seemed to serve a more decorative function and to provide the occasional note of glitter on a table that might otherwise be somber. Most of the pieces were for the center of the table or the sideboard. One problem was technical since footed pieces were a challenge, but had the demand existed the inventive glassmakers would have found the way to supply it.

*Cup Plates*

A fascinating group of the wares are cup plates,

which were made to place cups on while the saucer was used for drinking. These must have had strong popular appeal. They were made in purely decorative patterns and timely commemorative designs. Obvious subjects like George Washington, the American Eagle, and one of the first frigates of the infant United States Navy, the U.S.S. *Constitution*, were used as well as emblems of political campaigns. Other popular subjects were the Log Cabin, the Cider Barrel, Henry Clay, and William Henry Harrison, the singer Jenny Lind, the Bunker Hill Monument and the steamship *Chancellor Livingston*. Many of these are known in more than one version. Popular themes were frequently redone or copied by competitors.

For collectors esthetics and rarity combine to determine desirability. The small plates were made in quantity and the differences on absolutely esthetic grounds are broad, but there is a certain amount of repetition in effect. The collector takes account of every detail and finds the variations of the same design that show it was made in more than one mold. The careful observation of detail leads to discoveries that help fill in the missing chapters of the history of this field, but they also make cup plate collecting a little like stamp collecting.

*Lamps and Candlesticks*

In lamps and candlesticks there was less of a tendency to keep to the lacy surfaces. Many of the early pieces are made up of contrasting smooth parts with fussier sections of Lacy Glass. Cup plate molds were sometimes utilized to form bases in ingenious combinations. Lamps entirely of pressed glass made in separate parts joined as they came out of the molds were introduced in the 1830s, but the greater quantity appear to have been later, because they are simpler in design.

Blown and pressed candlestick. An interesting combination of techniques. Boston and Sandwich Glass Company, about 1825. *The Brooklyn Museum Collection.*

*The Move
Toward
Simplification*

The 1840s marked a change in taste. The intricate designs of the 1830s were simplified. The shift was propitious because it was no longer economically feasible to make molds with all the details used in the 1830s. Conservative repetitions of designs of earlier decades become disappointing in the '40s because backgrounds are left bare and the glitter is lacking. In the more original work the effect is grander and the work is bolder. The metal was improved and colors were more frequently used, so that the intricacy of the mold was no longer needed to cover up shortcomings in the glass. For candlesticks and lamps, the designs are often more classical in spirit. Columnar forms were popular in designs that once more were conceived in terms of the handsome outline rather than being dependent on detail. The

Left to right: White opaque glass caryatid candlestick by Boston and Sandwich Glass Company, about 1850; Opalescent glass sugar bowl, Ashburton pattern, made in Cambridge, Massachusetts, and Pittsburgh, 1850–1880; Yellow and opalescent glass dolphin candlestick, Pittsburgh, circa 1860. *The Metropolitan Museum of Art: Gift of Emily W. Miles, 1946.*

Compote with representation of Jenny Lind as pedestal. American, 1850. *The Brooklyn Museum Collection.*

1840s marked the introduction of the popular dolphin design which remained a favorite for several decades. Often colored glass and sometimes opaque whites, blues, and greens were used for the dolphin candlesticks. Besides being made at Sandwich and the New England Glass Company, Pittsburgh glass-houses such as McKee Brothers were producing simi-lar work. A technical improvement made it possible to produce candlesticks in a single mold. This may have taken place in the '50s, but no proof has been discovered. The one-section mold was used for a variety of new designs including the caryatid and crucifix sticks associated with Sandwich.

*Patterned*
*Tablewares*

The simple approach also was used for vases, spills, sugar bowls, and toilet bottles. The period marked the introduction of tablewares in sets of a particular pattern. There is a good chance that the sets were made as early as the late 1830s. Each pattern was named, and collectors today apply names that are sometimes original and sometimes not, depending upon whether or not the original name was known when the pattern first appeared. Names were some-times purely descriptive, such as Raised Diamond and Sharp Diamond. Other times the reasons are more complex and designs were called Ashburton, Colonial, Union, and the like. Popular patterns were frequently pirated, or, to put it more politely, be-came common property. The Pittsburgh and New England glasshouses were the largest, but others also competed. Some of the designs of the '40s and '50s were in demand as late as the 1870s but another change had begun by 1860.

*Reaction Back*
*to Fussiness*

The changes in style are sometimes like the swinging of a pendulum. Action brings reaction, but the shift-ing is a back-and-forth movement rather than a progression of any kind. Lacy glass had been fussy and then in the '40s pressed glass had become relatively plain. In the '60s the fussy was again in demand. It wasn't the same style that was revived, but a new repertory of designs to achieve the glit-

Pair of celery vases and a covered compote, thumbprint or argus pattern.
Bakewell, Pears and Company, Pittsburgh, 1860–1870. *The Metropolitan
Museum of Art: Gift of Emily Winthrop Miles.*

ter of the earlier product. The changes in manufacturing procedure meant that molds had to be
less intricate and costly, but also the patterns favored
were more naturalistic than the stylized designs of
the 1830s. There are various fruit and floral motifs
on backgrounds that are frequently ribbed or otherwise patterned. Cut glass and the earlier designs
were the inspiration for occasional examples, but
when drapery and garland motifs were used more
often the rendering was as realistic as the mold al-
lowed. More than three hundred patterns popular
in the period between about 1850 and 1890 were
listed in Ruth Webb Lee's pioneer study of pressed
glass. The period was one of extreme competition
and compromise. Flint glass was replaced by a lime
glass that was less costly in the 1860s and although
the lime glass was not as resonant it did have the
same brilliance as the higher quality product. Lime

Left to right: Pressed-glass creamers, American, about 1870 in Lincoln drape, magnet and grape, and ribbed diamond patterns. *The Metropolitan Museum of Art: Gift of Emily Winthrop Miles.*

Left to right: Pressed-glass sugar bowls, American, 1860–1870 in pineapple, bellflower, and horn of plenty patterns. *Courtesy Helga Photographic Service, Kenneth B. Way.*

glass was introduced in 1864 by William Leighton at the West Virginia plant of Hobbs, Brockunier and Company and used in almost every major American glasshouse except New England Glass Company and Boston and Sandwich, with the latter finally switching before 1880.

Butter dish, coin pattern, American, about 1890. Made for Chicago Columbian Exposition of 1893. *The Brooklyn Museum Collection.*

Covered compote in westward-ho pattern. By James Gillinder & Sons, Philadelphia, Pennsylvania, about 1875. *The Brooklyn Museum Collection.*

*Variety in Late Pressed Glass*

Pressed glass of the nineteenth century is a field of variety. Late pressed glass was made in clear, colored, and opaque glass. In spite of an underlying theme of imitating cut glass, the requirements of the mold and the integrity of designers led to work that is distinctive. The field reflects three tendencies —the lacy, the bold and simple, and the late, which is mildly intricate and naturalistic—which follow a chronological sequence for beginning but do not disappear when succeeded by a new tendency. The

Opaque white pressed-glass covered dish. Probably Mc-Kee Brothers, Pittsburgh, about 1890. *Chrysler Museum Institute of Glass.*

Purple marble glass candlesticks and platter. Once attributed to Challinor, Taylor and Company, Tarentum, Pennsylvania, about 1880, now considered English. *The Metropolitan Museum of Art: Gift of Emily Winthrop Miles, 1946.*

last, made widely and very competitively is sometimes most open to question on the matter of integrity of design, but that question is best answered by the collectors or students observing the pieces. Imitation cut-glass slippers, glass shoes attached to roller skates, dogs pulling carts, and sleighs or carriages to serve as toothpick holders seem a bit difficult to categorize in a survey of the nineteenth-century decorative arts. Pressed glass is the medium in which problems in taste are blatantly manifested; it was created a luxury available to all, and was often designed to attract the casual buyer rather than the serious esthetician.

# CHAPTER XI

# Art Glass

Art glass is ornamental glass, made to be decorative rather than functional. It was made to look expensive by appearing to require special virtuosity. As an American phenomenon it dates primarily from the 1880s to the present day. Several types of decorative glass, however, were introduced before art glass came into fashion.

*The Precedents of Art Glass*   By the 1840s the New England Glass Company and Brooklyn Flint Glass Company were producing fine wares that proved the talents of their skilled craftsmen. Their output included paperweights, with intricate three-dimensional designs which had become fashionable in France by the 1840s and not much later were being made in New England and New York. Nicholas Lutz, who had worked at St. Louis in France, where paperweights of the best type were made, did fine examples for Sandwich with miniature fruit on a striped or latticinio background. John Gilliland of the Brooklyn Flint Glass Company made faceted paperweights with colored-glass overlay bordering the opening on each side through which the small floral decoration, known as millefiori, could be seen. Others were made in the shape of apples and pears. At Millville, New Jersey, a rough flower decoration was used with a

Paperweight. By W. T. Gillinder and Sons, Philadelphia, about 1860. *Collection of the Philadelphia Museum of Art.*

Paperweight. American, late nineteenth century. *Philadelphia Museum of Art: The Elizabeth Wandell Smith Collection.*

less than perfect glass weight. The range of American weights is broad in both approach and date. Some relatively recent examples are very much in the spirit of the late nineteenth century.

Silvered glass, an imitation of silver achieved by putting mercury in between layers of glass, was developed at midcentury for decorative pieces such as drapery tiebacks and vases. The silvered pieces are an interesting attempt at diversity developed at the moment Bohemian glass was being made by the larger glasshouses.

*Special Color*
*Effects*

More appropriate to the name are the late blown and pressed pieces in special colors that were made after the Civil War. They were made as expensive luxuries and meant to appeal to the fast-growing group of the middle class seeking new decorative work for their homes. The eastern factories were attracted to answering the new demand because they had craftsmen who were skilled and the raw materials for making fine glass, at a time when western competition was reducing the demand for their table-wares in the growing market. Art glass was made to show off the skills of the makers and the pocketbooks of the patrons. It was generally designed in the vocabulary or ornament that is derived from Middle Eastern and Oriental sources. No special interest in preserving the integrity of the glass was evinced, but rather it became a medium for startling effects of all kinds, with the glass simulating porcelain or metal at times.

*Colored Glass*
*Refined*

The phenomenon came into its own in about 1880 when the finer glasshouses began competing in the manufacture of colored glass. Varicolored glass was made in forms that were often exotic. The first type to be introduced in a succession was Amberina. It is a glass that is transparent and shades from red on top to yellow on bottom. It was made at the New England Glass Company under a patent of 1883 (the name was trademarked in 1884), but Mount Washington Glass put out a very similar product trademarked in 1886 as Rose Amber. Amberina was made in blown and molded wares. The West Virginia glasshouse Hobbs, Brockunier and Company obtained a license to make it in 1886, and that same year New England Glass patented a variation, Plated Amberina, which had an opaque opal inner lining. Amberina was popular and imitated widely with variations made in France and England.

*Opaque Glass Improved*

Mat-finish opaque glass molded in simple over-all patterns such as quilting and herringbone was introduced in the United States shortly after 1880. An 1881 patent to William Dean and Alphonse Peltier was for this type of glass, which collectors call Satinware, Pearl Satinware, or Mother of Pearl. By whatever name it is called, the ware is often shaded in color like Amberina, but not always. It is frequently decorated in enamel or beads. Mount Washington Glass was a prime producer, but again, the ware was not exclusively theirs although the patent had been assigned to them.

Opaque glass in exotic colors was known in a number of other variations. Burmese and Peachblow are two that were very popular and made by many glasshouses in spite of efforts by patentees to

Group of Amberina glass covered bowls, a tumbler and a mug. By the New England Glass Works, William L. Libbey and Son, Proprietors, Cambridge, Massachusetts, about 1885. *The Metropolitan Museum of Art: Gift of Emily Winthrop Miles.*

A collection of "Hobnail" glass of a type made at many American glass-houses, circa 1880. *The Metropolitan Museum of Art: Gift of Emily Winthrop Miles.*

A selection of satin glass in various patterns. American, circa 1890. *The Metropolitan Museum of Art: Gift of Emily Winthrop Miles, 1946.*

protect their property. The forms were sometimes exotic, but more often popular they were eclectic shapes decorated in what must have been the average man's dream of artistic pattern. Peachblow is particularly interesting because the inspiration was

a Chinese porcelain vase that had become the subject of much conversation when it brought $18,000
at the auction of Mrs. Mary Morgan's collection.
The Morgan vase was called Peach bloom, so Peachblow was a simple variation of the term. There
were imitations of the original Chinese porcelain
piece made by New England Glass and Hobbs,
Brockunier, but the ware in both glossy and mat
finish was made by many companies. Shaded from
pink to a very soft pale rose, it is thought that the
coloring was offered earlier as Wild Rose. A variation of Peachblow called Agata had the mottling
of the porcelain.

The opaque pale-colored and shaded glass served
as the ground for a variety of decorative motifs,
most of which were applied in relief. Gold was
popular for this, but thick enamel and beads were
used in different ways to create a poor man's
jeweled Sèvres, which had been high fashion a
short time earlier.

"Agata" vase, a variation of Peachblow.
The New England Glass Works. *The
Brooklyn Museum Collection.*

*Overlay Glass*

Among the types of art glass that show skill and opulence, overlay is one that seems to be either a good joke or an example of great artistry, depending upon the viewer. It was made widely and appealed strongly in its day. Overlay is opaque glass to which glass decoration is applied. The shapes are varied, but often they are the same exotic types that were used for other art glass. Fruit and flowers on vines are a favored subject for the applied work. The effect is a bit like that of cake decoration, but the glass is less easy to handle than icing. Overlay may very well symbolize art glass in its use of the exotic and the familiar for obviously virtuoso work.

*Exotic Effects Sought*

The tendencies of the art glass designers may be contrasted in other ways. The exotic was emphasized in pale colors and delicate designs admired at the time. This tendency is exemplified by Pomona, a design with a pale warm gray-white rough-surfaced ground created by acid staining. This ground set off enamel floral decoration. The original process, patented by Joseph Locke for the New England Glass Company in 1885, was expensive to produce. A less brilliant and less expensive variant was introduced, and the two known as "first grind" and

Blown, engraved cased bowl of opaque pink over white, about 1880–1890. *The Brooklyn Museum Collection.*

Pair of vases of overlay glass. West Virginia or New England, circa 1890. *Chrysler Museum Institute of Glass.*

Tumbler of "Pomona" glass. The New England Glass Company, about 1885. *The Brooklyn Museum Collection.*

Latticinio vase, attributed to Nicholas Lutz. The Boston and Sandwich Glass Company, about 1880. *The Brooklyn Museum Collection.*

"second grind" are distinguished by collectors. Virtuoso work based on more spectacular historical examples is seen in a group of techniques which involved making varicolored glass like one type of ancient Venetian glass. Gold, or a number of colors, would be used to make Vasa Murrhina, Spatter or Spangled glass that is difficult to attribute to a specific glasshouse. Still another type of American glass that brings a specific approach to mind is Mary Gregory, which is a dark-colored transparent glass decorated with white enamel painted figures. Essentially a popularized version of the more elaborate cameo glass which was rarely attempted in America, Mary Gregory was one of the many decorators responsible for this kind of decoration at Sandwich. The subjects are children playing and the approach was anything but restricted to Sandwich or Mary Gregory.

As a popular vehicle, art glass tended to follow the taste of the times. At its height in a period of searching and inquiry for design, the glass reflects the floundering in impressive and pretty designs. As a commercial product, art glass was meant for a large market.

*Art Glass*
*Comes of Age*

In complete contrast to the usual art glass is Louis Comfort Tiffany's glass. First of all, he used glass as a true art medium, designing to please himself in the hope that what he liked would appeal to others.

*Louis Comfort*
*Tiffany*

Louis Comfort Tiffany was born in 1848, the son of Charles Tiffany, head of the famous New York jewelry shop. He studied painting with George Inness and worked in Paris. Attracted to the decorative arts, he experimented with making stained

Collection of Favrile glass by Louis Comfort Tiffany. American, 1895–1915. *Chrysler Museum Institute of Glass.*

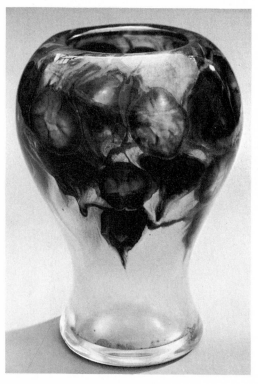

Favrile glass vase by Louis Comfort Tiffany. American, 1913. *The Metropolitan Museum of Art: Gift of the Louis Comfort Tiffany Foundation, 1951.*

Favrile glass bowl by Louis Comfort Tiffany, American. *The Metropolitan Museum of Art: Gift of the Louis Comfort Tiffany Foundation, 1951.*

Reddish brown Tiffany Favrile glass flower vase decorated with a peacock feather pattern in conventional colors, circa 1900. *The Brooklyn Museum Collection.*

glass, and became interested in interior decorating. After 1892 he worked on blown glass, and in 1896 was showing in a famous Paris shop, S. Bing's Art Nouveau. There his work was exhibited with that of the best European artist-craftsmen who were attempting to start a new style that reintegrated the decorative arts and painting. Tiffany's shop produced glass in many different designs—all fresh and forthright. Technically facile, the products are subtle in their display of virtuosity. Thin elongated forms tend to be more common than others, but Middle Eastern and Oriental models were the frequent sources of inspiration for shapes. Iridescence is almost a Tiffany signature, but there were many examples that are plain. In Tiffany work the single rule was to work with quality and integrity and the results rarely look routine until the late efforts. Tiffany called his glass Favrile, according to a brochure he published in 1896, for the name was said to come from an Old English word, "fabrile," meaning "belonging to a craftsman or his craft." Not long afterward, Tiffany offered an explanation for the term as one easy to pronounce and remember, based on the German word for color, *Farbe*. Tiffany made ornamental vases as well as tablewares in finely conceived designs that borrowed nothing from the more ordinary American glass of the period. The work was often signed by scratching the name or initials and a coded number on the glass. Also paper labels inscribed Tiffany Favrile Glass were used. Both methods of identification have been faked frequently.

*Attempts to Commercialize Tiffany*

There were many who attempted to adapt Tiffany's ideas to more commercial work. European as well as American glasshouses imitated the iridescent glass in elongated exotic forms. The Austrian manufacturer, Loetz, used iridescence on shapes of Middle Eastern inspiration, but the results never seemed as individual, and the accidental look of asymmetry in Tiffany glass becomes strangely premeditated in the Austrian imitation. The Quezal Art Glass and Decorating Company also did work based on the Tiffany approach. In its efforts the regularity is more frank and the results seem a fine adaptation of the freer models to meet factory requirements. The same effect was achieved in the Tiffany-like ware made by the Union Glass Company and labeled "Kew Blas." The efforts that relate to the Art Nouveau style and reflect the innovations of Tiffany continued into the 1920s. Victor Durand made art wares at his Vineland, New Jersey, shop that were distinctive but still depended on Tiffany for basic ideas. The Imperial Glass Company and Fenton Art Glass also did work that was in the same spirit at that time. Steuben Glass included a line called Aurene which exploited iridescence and at the same time is in the spirit of Durand. The art director at Steuben from 1903 to 1934, Frederick Carder, was an important figure in twentieth-century art glass. His own innovations were in relief ornamented glass of several sorts. He did a variation of cameo glass early and revived an ancient technique of high relief, Diatreta, later.

With the exception of Tiffany, the glass that is called art glass is a commercial decorative ware made primarily for sale. There has been little effort in glass to investigate to see if craftsmen working in the arts and crafts tradition produced significant glass.

# CHAPTER XII

# Functional Collectibles

Bottles are a category of glass that falls between the functional and the decorative. Designed as functional containers for the storage of liquids, their shapes have been determined by appearance as well as utilitarian objectives through the years. Even the shapes of ordinary wine and spirit bottles made of dark green glass changed every few years in the seventeenth and eighteenth centuries. Smaller flasks for spirits or perfumes were generally ornamented by being made in a mold, engraved, or painted. In the early nineteenth century the introduction of the one-piece mold for bottlemaking affected shapes and provided a new approach to decorative wares. Later in the nineteenth century bottles became one of the prime mediums for that strange phenomenon advertising art which has the popular appeal of folk art combined with the facile skills of academic art to create very sentimental styles. For collectors today all bottles are of interest and many have been concentrating on the more recent examples which continue the trends of the last century.

*Wine and*
*Spirit Bottles*

American wine and spirit bottles of the seventeenth and eighteenth centuries are hard to identify. Shapes show age and generally in the early examples the seal on a bottle would include the initials or name of the owner and the date the bottle was made or the liquid in it was sealed. When the bottle can be identified as the property of an American it is often assumed that it was made at one of the

American glasshouses; but Americans imported wines and liquors, sometimes bottled. The group that are considered American follow the evolution in shape outlined for English bottles. Roughly speaking, the earliest type, and one found at Rhode Island Indian grave excavations, is short and squat, almost globular, with a broad neck about half as high as the body itself. One example is dated 1724. The 1752 bottle owned by the Philadelphia cabinetmaker William Savery was very probably made at the Wistar glasshouse. It is cylindrical in body and thinner proportionately. As time went on, bottles generally were made thinner and taller. There are many exceptions to the rules, however, and the globular shape of the seventeenth and early eight-

Bottle made for William Savery. Possibly made by Caspar Wistar, about 1750. *Collection of the Philadelphia Museum of Art.*

eenth century was continued for all of the eighteenth century and into the nineteenth century in thinner glass and lighter proportions. Examples of the type were made at the Ohio glasshouses as well as in New Hampshire during the nineteenth century. There are English versions referred to as Hogarth bottles. Since still another source of the type was a glasshouse in Ludlow, Massachusetts, the type is referred to as a Ludlow bottle by some, and, because of the shape, small versions have been called Chestnut bottles by others. Whatever it is called it was a simple form used through a good part of the nineteenth century at glasshouses all over the country.

Green glass bottle. Possibly by Stiegel, 1765. *Courtesy, Henry Francis du Pont Winterthur Museum.*

Left to right: Bottle, by A. R. Samuels, Philadelphia, Pennsylvania, 1855–1870; Flask with Masonic emblems, by Marlboro Street Works, Keene, New Hampshire, about 1820; "Union" design flask by Coventry Glass Works, Coventry, Connecticut, about 1845. *The Metropolitan Museum of Art, Purchase 1910, The Rogers Fund.*

*Smaller Containers*

Smaller bottles for snuff, medicine, shoe blacking, or other salable liquids were sometimes plain because information was on the paper label originally attached. By the beginning of the nineteenth century the inscription was also in the glass. These bottles were made clear, amber, or green.

*Uses of Expand-Mold Glass*

The eighteenth-century scent bottles and flasks were decorated in relief patterns by making them in expand-molds. These were produced by Stiegel, Amelung, the Connecticut glasshouses, and in the Midwest as late as 1850. The blown three-mold technique was used for similar flasks and bottles made at a variety of places in the 1820–1850 period. Another decorative type that was blown and popular in American glasshouses is the Gemel bottle. A two-

Flask, representing Benjamin Franklin. By Kensington Glass Works, Philadelphia, Pennsylvania, about 1835. *Collection of the Philadelphia Museum of Art.*

sectioned or twin bottle, these were often made to look like bellows. They often had applied glass borders and bodies made of looped glass. Made mainly in the first half of the nineteenth century, they were probably designed for display and not use.

By about 1815 the use of the full-size molds for making bottles enabled the manufacturers to use inscribed names and relief decoration. Cologne bottles made in various colors are good examples of how the sides of bottles could be decorated in floral, scroll, or more complex motifs. Architectural details were used along with a variety of shapes. Shell, banjo, and violin forms are typical. The glass was generally transparent and colored, but occasionally opaque white.

*Molded Whiskey Flasks*    Whiskey flasks made in the full-size molds date from about 1815 to 1850. They can be divided into groups relating to the decorative schemes. Generally regarded as the earliest are those with simple sunburst decoration made at Zanesville, Ohio, and the Marlboro Street glasshouse, Keene, New Hampshire.

*Emblems on Bottles*

The Masons were significant enough to inspire decoration on many different objects. Flasks with the emblems were produced by eastern and western glasshouses between 1815 and 1830, mainly. There seems to have been a decline in demand after that.

Patriotic symbols were another logical subject on flasks. Columbia surrounded by stars, the Flag, and most popular of all, the American Eagle were featured on examples that vary in date and geographical origin. The New London Glass Works made Eagle flasks in the 1860s. Extending the concept of patriotism one step further another group of motifs suggest the progress and prosperity of the young Republic. Railroads were shown, along with corn, rye, wheat, and ships with slogans such as "Corn for the World," "Successes to the Railroad," and the more immediate reminder "Use me but do not abuse Me."

*Portrait Flasks*

Portrait flasks were also popular and the choice of subject included national heroes, celebrities, and presidential candidates. The heroes are in the main easily recognizable. Washington was a favorite subject, Franklin much less frequently encountered. Lafayette, De Witt Clinton, Major Samuel Ringgold, a Mexican War hero, Lajos Kossuth, a Hungarian revolutionary hero, and Jenny Lind are among those shown. The presidential candidates include as unlikely a person for a whiskey flask as John Quincy Adams, who appears on one of the earliest. Andrew Jackson, the poor man's friend, Zachary Taylor, Henry Clay, and President Harrison were among the

Olive green flask. Marlboro Street Works, Keene, New Hampshire, about 1825. *The Brooklyn Museum Collection.*

portraits represented on campaign flasks. One of the last series of flasks to be made bears the legend "Pikes Peak or Bust" and celebrates the gold rush of 1858. These were made as late as 1870.

In the flasks there was little variation in shape. The sides generally tapered out to curving shoulders with a very short neck. The flasks were thin and held about a pint or half a pint. They were made in the New Jersey glasshouses that carried on traditions begun by Wistar, and at a variety of other glasshouses all over the country. Often designs were pirated by casting molds from a bottle so that without a mark it is hard to attribute an example, because almost identical bottles might be made by several manufacturers.

A small but interesting group is in the form of cabins. Some were made at the time of the Harrison campaign, but most famous of all, the Booze

Above left: Mineral water bottle, for "Poland Waters, H. Ricker & Sons, proprietor." American, about 1900. *The Brooklyn Museum Collection.* Above right: Clear glass filled with sand souvenir paperweight representing Gay Head Lighthouse, Massachusetts. American, about 1890. *The Brooklyn Museum Collection.*

bottle made for a liquor dealer who probably borrowed the appropriate name to suit his venture, was made in about 1860 by the Whitney Bottle Company at Glassboro, New Jersey.

*Bitters Bottles*    A later approach is to be found after the 1860s. The extensive group of bottles in the form of figures or small objects is often referred to as bitters bottles. Some were undoubtedly used for the nostrums that were called bitters, and others filled different needs. The bottles were often patented and always distinctive. One early example was in the form of an Indian princess for "Brown's Celebrated Indian Herb Bitters." Patented in 1868 this was popular for some time. Others took the form of objects like frankfurters and cigars. The bottle for Poland Springs Mineral Water is in the form of an old bearded man, "Moses at the Spring." The range seems almost infinite and designing them continues. Enthusiastic bottle collectors don't stop at a particular date but acquire the most recent examples that show disinctiveness, if not distinction.

# Index